The Environment

and the Christian

The Environment

and the Christian

What Does the New Testament Say

about the Environment?

Edited by

Calvin B. DeWitt

BAKER BOOK HOUSE
Grand Rapids, Michigan 49516

Library of Congress Cataloging-in-Publication Data

The Environment and the Christian: what does the New Testament say
  about the environment? / edited by Calvin B. DeWitt.
            p.   cm.
      Includes bibliographical references and indexes.
      ISBN 0-8010-3006-4
          1. Human ecology—Religious aspects—Christianity. 2. Jesus Christ—
  Person and offices. 3. Bible.—N.T.—Criticism, interpretation, etc.
  I. DeWitt, Calvin B.
  BT695.5.E585   1991
  261.8'362—dc20
                                                                      91-20482
                                                                           CIP

Printed on recycled paper

Contents

84362

Preface

Proper care and keeping of creation is a growing concern of Christians. As we learn more and more about the degradation and destruction of our Lord's earth, we also are giving deep thought to our responsibilities before God as stewards of earth and its creatures. In the 1980s many of us refreshed ourselves in the biblical teachings on responsibility toward the creation. In the process we discovered the Bible to be a rich source of teaching in this area. Some of us came to see God's Holy Word as a kind of ecological book—a manual helping believers to live rightly on earth—a manual that would help us "so live on earth that heaven would not be a shock to us."

Through our reading of Scripture in this time of renewed concern for God's earth, we have been renewed with a fulfilling richness. We are assured and strengthened in its teachings, namely, God is Creator of the whole universe (Gen. 1:1)—a universe that speaks eloquently of the Creator (Ps. 19), and God is owner of all creation (Deut. 10:14; Ps. 24:1; 1 Cor. 10:26)—a creation that God sustains and loves, giving water and food to all creatures (Ps. 104; Acts 14:17), as well as giving Christ Jesus (John 3:16). We are reaffirmed that the Lord blesses us and *keeps* us (Ps. 104; Num. 6:24–26).

But we are also challenged. We have found that we too are expected to *keep* the earth (Gen. 2:15). As the Lord keeps us, so are we to keep God's creation. In keeping the earth and its creatures, we are to give ourselves, other creatures, and the land their Sabbath rests—their times for restoration, their times for enjoying the fruits of God's creation (Exod. 20, 23; Lev. 25, 26). As God provides for the creatures, so must we—allowing them also to "be fruitful and increase in number" (Gen. 1:22, 28; 8:17; 9:1, 7), and not "add house to house and join field to field" until only humans occupy the land (Isa. 5:8). And, if we accept Noah's dedication to God's will as our own example, we should spare no expense of time, money, and reputation to save species threatened with extinction (Gen. 6:19–20).

We are challenged not to defile or pollute God's gifts in creation. While expected to enjoy creation's blessings responsibly, we must not diminish its fruitfulness. Our Lord asks, "Is it not enough for you to feed on the good pasture? Must you also trample the rest of your pasture with your feet. Is it not enough for you to drink clear water? Must you also muddy the rest with your feet? Must my flock feed on what you have trampled and drink what you have muddied with your feet?" (Ezek. 34:18–19).

Given the many things that the Bible has taught us in this time of renewed environmental awareness, some Christians have begun to ask, "What is distinctively 'Christian' about these biblical teachings?" Others say, "Nearly every verse that is cited, and nearly every interpretation of the Scripture on environmental stewardship is based on Old Testament sources. If this material is only from the Old Testament, is it relevant for us today? What is 'Christian' about Christian environmental stewardship?"

This book attempts to answer these questions. It confirms that the New Testament does offer a distinctively Christian contribution to environmental stewardship. While not pushing aside the Old Testament, this book finds and addresses the specific offerings of the New Testament to Christian environmental stewardship. And it shows these contributions to be substantial and of significant consequence.

Some Christian churches and denominations have referred to themselves as "New Testament churches," and some derive most of their teachings and practices from the New Testament. Others draw upon both Old and New Testaments, but are committed to a distinctively Christian witness not only in their profession of Jesus Christ, but also in their dealing with environmental issues. It is to these churches and their people that this book attempts to be particularly sensitive and helpful. It is also addressed, however, to a wider Christian and world community—to evangelical and mainline churches, to Christian colleges, and to students. And it is addressed to any and all who believe that religion has a legitimate place in addressing the very serious ethical and practical problems we face today in relation to environmental degradation, ecological "sustainability," and human responsibility.

To the secular reader who wishes to tap the resources of the Christian faith, much will be found here. Especially, one will find that not only is the environmental crisis a religious one, but that religion has important contributions to make toward the reversal of environmental destruction and the establishment of ecological sustainability.

To those who have been attracted to the New Age movement and see it as the answer to their quest for spiritual and environmental wholeness, you will find here a rich and full alternative. Much has been written and believed over thousands of years about this "new age," a "new age" that in the Scriptures is called the "kingdom of God." In an essay entitled "Two Economies," Wendell Berry asked what kind of economy would be comprehensive enough to prevent ruination of farmland. To this Wes Jackson responded, "the kingdom of God." In explicating Wes Jackson's answer Berry observed that "the first principle of the Kingdom of God is that it includes everything; in it, the fall of every sparrow is a significant event. . . .

Another principle, both ecological and traditional, is that everything in the Kingdom of God is joined both to it and everything else that is in it."[1]

This book has something to say about the kingdom of God. It has something to say about following the Second Adam. By saying this, and more, it is intended as a guidepost that brings renewed reflection on the current wave of environmental and spiritual awareness—in the light of the New Testament, in the Light of the world.

Au Sable Institute of Environmental Studies is here acknowledged for supporting the Forum from which this book is derived, and for supporting the preparation of this manuscript. The Au Sable Forums have been conducted by the Institute since 1980, bringing theologians, scientists, and laypeople together to explore the relationships between the Scriptures and environment, between Christianity and ecology. Numerous articles and books have resulted from these Forums. Thanks go to all who have contributed to them and for steadily building a base of knowledge in this vital area. Many people who write in the area of Christianity and ecology—as Forum participants, professors, or students—have come to the Au Sable Institute, and many of them consider it a kind of second home. Through the Institute's association with some eighty evangelical Christian colleges and universities throughout the United States and Canada, and by its associations with Christian and religious leaders worldwide, it has provided a place and an opportunity for the integration of faith and learning on matters relating to the integrity of creation.

For supporting this project through a generous Trustees Grant, thanks go to the Institute's Board of Trustees, namely, John D. Loeks, Orin G. Gelderloos, Harold Z. Snyder, Bert Froysland, John Olmstead, Ghillean T. Prance, Ross S. Whaley, J. Elliot. Corbett, and the late James Justafson.

Also acknowledged is the invaluable and selfless service of J. Mark Thomas. As a Senior Research Fellow of

Au Sable Institute and an accomplished scholar and writer in social and environmental ethics, he worked closely and continuously with the editor through all phases of the preparation of the manuscript, including text reading, editing, correspondence, and proofreading. Without his energetic work and devotion to this task, this book would not have been produced.

Finally, thanks go to Baker Book House and its staff who published this work.

Calvin DeWitt
Editor

Introduction

Seven Degradations of Creation

Calvin B. DeWitt

A crisis of degradation is enveloping earth. Never before have human beings wielded so much power over creation. The ever increasing population—now 5.2 billion—combines with the ability of humans to amplify muscular strength with instruments that press earth's immense energy systems into our service, making humans a formidable force. If the governing ethic of human action were that "the earth is the Lord's and all that it contains," if human beings resolved to *bless* and *keep* the creation as the Creator *blesses* and *keeps* people, if human actions were to affirm the long-standing belief that avarice and greed are vices, and if we asked "What is right?" before decisions were made, then perhaps there would be no crisis.

What degradations are brought on creation by the human assault? What response might a religious ethic make to such degradations? Some have pointed to a Christian response to this crisis, primarily using Old Testament sources.[1] But Christianity is rooted in the New Testament as well as the Old Testament. In fact, the New Testament forms the distinct scriptural basis for what has become the Christian faith. Since the New Testament is so basic to Christianity, it is necessary to consider its teachings if there is to be any serious development of an explicitly *Christian* response to creation's degradation. Building on New Testament sources, the essayists in this volume accomplish just this task, offering insights into a Christian response to environmental destruction, insights that point to hope.

After a description of each of the seven degradations of creation, this introductory essay will cite several Old Testament passages to recall several contributions of the Hebrew Scriptures to an understanding of Christian environmental stewardship. Subsequently, the question will be asked, "What does the New Testament teach that will help us respond to this degradation?" As a student of bogs, marshes, mires, and swamps, I know the feeling of the place we stand, of the nature of our journey together: We are uncertain travelers on uncertain ground. But the study of such uncertain areas is the stuff of which research is made, wherein exploration is truly challenging and exciting. Accordingly, this inquiry does not have a path set clearly before us. New ground is being tread.

The collection of essays in this book presents various approaches that can be used to address the contributions of the New Testament to Christian environmental stewardship. They express insights into a correct assessment of the contributions of the New Testament—in the light of the whole of Scripture—to understanding the environmental crisis that is upon us.

Land Conversion and Habitat Destruction

Since 1850, 2.2 billion acres of natural lands have been converted to human uses. This compares to earth's 16 billion acres that have some kind of vegetation (another 16 billion acres being ice, snow, and rock), and a current world cropland of 3.6 billion acres. Names given for this conversion of natural ecosystems include deforestation (forests), drainage or "reclamation" (wetlands), irrigation (arid and semiarid ecosystems), and plowing (grasslands and prairies). The most extensive conversion underway is tropical deforestation at an annual rate of twenty-five million acres (an area the size of Indiana). The immensity of this destruction bespeaks our power to alter the face of earth, harvesting forests we have not sown, destroying species not yet named, producing plywood and bathroom tissue from their substance, growing hamburger meat on the cleared land, destroying long-term sustainability of soils, forest creatures, and people. In the United States remnant woodlots and their creatures are replaced with parking lots, buildings, and additions to homes, offices, and churches. Of 400 million acres of cropland we have allotted for agriculture in the United States, three million are converted yearly to urban uses. Fields for grazing and crops no longer are "carved" from forests, they *replace* the forests; houses replace the best cropland. In the Old Testament, Isaiah warned, "Woe to you who add house to house and join field to field, till no space is left and you live alone in the land."[2]

Given the explicit concern of the Hebrew Scriptures for the responsible use of land, what does the New Testament add to this teaching, and how can it inform an effective response to the degradation caused by land conversion and habitat destruction?

Species Extinctions

Three species of creatures are extinguished *daily*. Their existence is cut off forever. Perhaps the rate is even much higher, since we do not know whether there are five million or forty million species of plants and animals on earth. While most temperate-zone species have been named, species in the tropics have not been named yet. Yet, named or unnamed, they appear in lumber yards as inexpensive plywood for our homes, offices, and boats, and in stores as lizard-skin wallets and shoes. Children around the world are given pennies to bring in skins of living creatures that will soon be worn as items of fashion. Expansions of homes and churches, elimination of the woodlot on the "back forty," and removal of vegetation once separating fields, add to the destruction. Even butterflies, once so common in the everyday life of city and country, are threatened by loss of habitat and herbicidal destruction of their food plants. Some people now urge people to plant butterfly gardens as a natural "ark" for preserving what otherwise might perish. Others urge preservation of remnant woodlots and prairies as natural "arks" in eager expectation that the deluge of people and their works will subside to find their proper bounds. (Even now, the churchyards of England are among the few remaining habitats for some creatures.) In the Old Testament the Creator said to Noah, "You are to bring into the ark two of all living creatures, male and female, to keep them alive with you."[3]

The Old Testament depicts the story of species preservation as the will of the Creator. What instruction of the New Testament guides our response to the threat of species extinctions?

Land Degradation

In much of the tall grass prairie (the "corn belt"), two bushels of topsoil are lost for every bushel of corn produced. Pesticides and herbicides have made it possible to plant corn, or any crop, year after year on the same land. Crop rotation (e.g., from corn to soy beans to alfalfa hay to pasture), was abandoned. Farmers became "free" to plant the same crop continuously and were often urged to do so by chemical manufacturers.

Also, farm animals could now be kept in feedlots and confinements, fencing and fence rows could be removed to allow for intensified use of the land, and losses of topsoil to wind and water erosion could be compensated by increasing fertilizer applications. What *could* be done *was* done, and the soil life was devastated. Today, earthworms no longer inhabit most farmland. Microscopic life of the soil has been severely altered. Birds have been diminished by the removal of fencerows and hedgerows that once separated the fields.

The land never rests; the creatures are driven off. The homes of the diverse creatures of the prairies, grasslands, forests, and fields have become chemical deserts. In the Torah the Lord warned, "When you enter the land I am going to give you, the land itself must observe a sabbath to the Lord," "But if you will not listen to me and carry out these commands . . . I will lay waste the land. . . . All the time that it lies desolate, the land will have the rest it did not have during the sabbaths you lived in it."[4]

The deep wisdom of the Old Testament includes reverence for the land. Does the New Testament add to this tradition?

Resource Conversion and Wastes and Hazards Production

Some seventy-thousand different chemicals have been created by our ingenuity. Unlike most chemicals made by organisms and geological processes of the creation, some of these chemicals leave life on earth defenseless. Among them are ones designed to destroy life, namely, biocides, pesticides, herbicides, avicides, and fungicides. Materials for producing these chemicals, such as petroleum and brines containing chlorine and fluorine, pose additional problems for life.

People have reworked large parts of the creation, making products, by-products, discards, and wastes. Every item in our homes, offices, churches, and industries, as well as each housing and commercial development we build, and every road we travel, are reworked parts of creation. For example, oil is shipped from Saudi Arabia to chemical plants, transformed into items like Styrofoam cups, which are used for beverages, discarded into the trash, trucked to a landfill, and then buried. During decomposition, some of the cup may enter the groundwater in the form of leachate, which may contaminate springs and wells, while other parts of the cup may enter the atmosphere as carbon dioxide, methane, and CFCs (chloroflourocarbons), which alter earth's energy exchange with the sun.

We live in a *flow-through economy*. It taps creation's wealth at one point and discards its transformations at another. Nature operates as a *cyclical economy* in which ecosystems sustain themselves by cycling materials. Regrettably, our economy is threatening the economy of creation. We interfere with creation's cycles on a grand scale, "trash" its creatures, pollute its waters, and mow down its plants. The Old Testament asks us, "Is it not enough for you to feed on the good pasture? Must you also trample the rest of your pasture with your feet? Is it not enough for you to drink clear water? Must you also muddy the rest with your feet?"[5]

If the Old Testament disapproves of the human despoliation of the environment, what does the New Testament teach regarding resource conversion and the production of wastes and hazards?

Global Toxification

A major feature of the earth's dynamic weather, ocean, and river systems is their transport and distribution of materials around the globe. Of the thousands of chemical substances we have created, hundreds have been injected into the atmosphere, discharged into rivers, and leaked into groundwater. Some have even joined global circulations. For example, some substances like DDT have appeared in antarctic penguins, while some biocides have been detected in a remote lake on Lake Superior's Isle Royale. Cancer has become pervasive in some herring gull populations.

In the interchange between creation's economy and ours, we face a planetary challenge. The consequences of what some call the "rape of the earth" are now widely experienced by many creatures. No longer is there merely a *local* environment affected by a *local* polluter. Global toxification is affecting all life, "all creatures, great and small," all people, rich and poor. The Old Testament says, "I brought you into a fertile land to eat its fruit and rich produce. But you came and defiled my land and made my inheritance detestable."[6]

That the land as given by God is good and fruitful, and not to be spoiled, is acknowledged by the Old Testament. So, how do the teachings of the New Testament inform a response to global toxification?

Alteration of Planetary Exchange

Fundamental to the processes that sustain life and earth's circulations of air and water is its exchange of energy with the sun and outer space. Earth's temperature depends upon the balance of energy received from the sun and energy reradiated to outer space. Carbon dioxide, methane, and twenty-five to thirty manufactured chemicals that have risen to the outer atmosphere of earth allow visible solar radiation to penetrate the atmosphere; these gases absorb energy reradiated by earth. Carbon dioxide and these synthetic chemicals, including CFCs, operate like the glass of a greenhouse, and thus are named "greenhouse gases." As car windshields allow sunlight to flow into cars but prevent reradiated infrared radiation to flow back, so the greenhouse gases trap heat. With the right concentration of these gases, earth retains enough heat to maintain the range of temperatures that we have experienced for centuries. As a result of deforestation, draining wetlands, and burning petroleum, coal, and wood, we have produced rising concentrations of atmospheric carbon dioxide, which allows less heat to escape back to outer space, thereby producing global warming. Adding to the effects of increasing carbon dioxide are other greenhouse gases produced by the chemical industry, such as refrigerants in air conditioners and refrigerators, CFCs from aerosol cans of paint and hair spray, Styrofoam, and some fire extinguishers. The earth's temperature has been rising very slowly over centuries, as is evidenced by melting snow caps and glaciers, and a slowly rising sea level. But now this rise will likely accelerate, with consequences not only for earth's temperature but also for the distribution of temperatures across the planet, with consequent changes in patterns of rainfall and drought.

CFCs operate not only as greenhouse gases. They also destroy the earth's ozone layer. Located in the outer atmosphere, this layer absorbs much of the sun's ultraviolet radiation, thereby protecting us from potential damage to genetic material in living creatures. The destruction of the ozone layer results in more ultraviolet light reaching creatures on earth, where it can cause (among other things) skin cancer in humans.

Consumption and production are now pursued on a scale that alters basic processes at the planetary level. The regulating and protective provisions of the creation are being destroyed. The Torah inquires, "Is this the way you repay the LORD, O foolish and unwise people? Is he not your Father, your Creator, who made you and formed you?"[7]

The ecological thrust of the Old Testament is clear. What more can be learned from the New Testament in responding to the challenges to life caused by the alteration of planetary exchange?

Human and Cultural Degradation

Among the most severe reductions of creation's richness is the degradation of cultures that have lived peaceably on the land for centuries. Many Amish and Mennonite farming communities operate under severe pressures of increased land taxes and encroaching urban development that push them to abandon their farms. The Amish of Lancaster County, Pennsylvania, are threatened by a proposed highway through the center of their 300-year-old, sustainable community. In the tropics, long-standing cultures living cooperatively with the forest are being wiped off the land by force, death, and legal procedures devised to deprive them of traditional lands. As they are extinguished, so are their rich heritages of unwritten knowledge. Successful ways of living in harmony with the land are forgotten. Names of otherwise undescribed forest creatures are lost. And uses of the wide array of tropical species for human food, fiber, and medicine are extinguished.

Not only is the great variety of natural species being diminished, but also the diversity of our agricultural heritage. Seeds of a wide variety of plants suited to small farms and gardens are displaced by new strains suited to mechanized planting and harvesting—strains uniform in color, size, and time of ripening. An aggressive economy—maximizing immediate return at the expense of sustainability—is sweeping the globe. Agri*culture* is being displaced by agri*business*.

In the name of conducting "good business," finding "sound" investments, and making "good" money, the powerful use the land and resources of the meek, depriving them of the ability to take care of themselves and the creation, depriving them of the inheritance of generations. Disconnected from land that could sustain them, they are driven into the cities, joblessness, and poverty. The Mosaic law warns, "Do not take advantage of each other. . . . The land must not be sold permanently, because the land is

mine and you are but aliens. . . ." The land must be
returned to the poor and the meek.[8]

The Lord observes that "Even the stork in the sky
knows her appointed seasons, and the dove, the swift and
the thrush observe the time of their migration," yet mar-
vels that "my people do not know the requirements of
the Lord."[9]

Concern for the flourishing of humanity and the earth
is clearly expressed in the Hebrew Scriptures. What,
then, does the New Testament contribute that might
inform a practical moral reaction to human and cultural
degradation?

The Response of the New Testament

In the midst of creation's garden—so abundantly yielding blessed fruits and supporting life in its God-declared
goodness—we have made the choice to extract more and
more, even at the expense of destroying creation's protective provisions and blessed fruitfulness. Before us the creatures fall—some diminished, some wiped clean from the
face of the Creator's canvas. We have chosen to trash the
great gallery of earth's Maker, replacing it with our own
creations "for the greatest good," creations that surpass
creation itself, creations "bigger than life." Under this
arrogant assault on the fabric of the biosphere, to use the
words of the Old Testament, "the earth dries up and with-
ers. . . . The earth is defiled by its people."[10]

What does the New Testament teach that would
help people to respond to this arrogant assault on the
biosphere?

We human beings make choices. Early on, we made the
choice to know good and evil. In the last several centuries
we have chosen to redefine the long-recognized vices of
avarice and greed as virtues. We have come to believe that
"looking out for number one" means getting more and
more for *self*. *Self*-interest, we now profess, is what brings

the greatest good. Choices made for the creation and the Creator have been usurped by choices made for *me*. The Old Testament says, "I have set before you life and death, blessings and curses. Now choose life, so that you and your children may live and that you may love the LORD your God, listen to his voice, and hold fast to him."[11]

Thus, in the broadest frame of reference, we must ask, What does the New Testament teach about choosing between life and death, between redemption and destruction, between restoration and degradation?

1

Christ as Creator and Redeemer

Loren Wilkinson

These are the questions before us: Is Jesus Christ Lord of the cosmos? Is Christ the Lord of personal life? Perhaps he is both. If so, how are the two lordships related? Is salvation through Jesus a personal transaction between individual human beings and their Creator? Does that reconciliation somehow involve the whole creation?

Creation and the "Cosmic Christ"

These are not theoretical questions from church history, abstract theology, or first-century mythology. They are absolutely central as we try to understand what the good news in Christ means, not only for individuals, but for a suffering creation. What, then, is the biblical teaching about the "cosmic Christ"?

The term "cosmic Christ" is not itself biblical, but the idea is close to the surface in so central a text as John 3:16: "For God so loved the world that he gave his one and only

25

son. . . ." Here the Greek word for "world" is *kosmos,* which here refers to the orderly totality of all things. It could be argued that the word refers to the human world, for the passage is followed immediately by descriptions of human response. But there are other indications in John's Gospel that Christ is Lord of the cosmos, the most sublime illustration being the simple declaration of the prologue: "In the beginning was the Word. . . . Through him all things were made" (John 1:1–3). The "all things" of that great declaration points clearly to the cosmic dimensions of Jesus' lordship, and allows us to expand "God so loved the world" to "God so loved the earth."

So by "cosmic Christ" we mean simply that the world to which God's Son came was not only the human world but the whole created earth—indeed, the universe. If this is so, then our understandings of the gospel, of eschatology, of "the new heaven and the new earth" must likewise include "all things."

Key New Testament Texts

Several crucial passages in the New Testament speak of this cosmic dimension of the gospel. We should review the main ones.

The most far-reaching verses may be the prologue to John's Gospel. We offer the following translation by Paulos Gregorios:

> At the source-spring of all, the Logos is and was. The Logos is God's vis-à-vis, and the Logos is God. It is this Logos that in the beginning was face to face with God. It is through the Logos that all existing things have come to exist. Without him not a single thing could have come into being. . . .[1]

Calling Jesus the Word who was with God at the beginning and saying that through him all things were made puts in the strongest possible terms the link between Jesus and the whole created cosmos. What is more, the use of the potent word "logos" links Jesus with the whole tradition of Greek cosmological speculation: Logos is the term that Heraclitus used to describe that which brings order to the flux of existence. The *spermatakoi logoi*, or seed words, are (according to the Stoics) those sparks of the world-soul which all individuals contain, and which enable them to act "according to nature." The logos is, according to the Alexandrian Jew, Philo, the first creation of God, by which God guides the world as by a rudder.[2] It is important to realize that these Hellenic speculations were the science, the "new ideas" of the day. Thus, to call Jesus the Logos in the cosmological context of these opening verses of John's Gospel is rather equivalent to speaking of him in terms of the unified field theory and the four (or is it now five?) forces. To call Jesus "the Word" is to link him with the most profound current speculations about the origin and nature of the cosmos.

The same sort of cosmic link is made in the opening verses of the Epistle to the Hebrews:

> In the past God spoke to our forefathers through the prophets at many times and in various ways, but in these last days he has spoken to us by his Son, whom he appointed heir of all things, and through whom he made the universe. The Son is the radiance of God's glory and the exact representation of his being, sustaining all things by his powerful word.
>
> (Heb. 1:1–3a)

Once again the starting point is human and personal, but the statement moves quickly from that human center to include the whole universe, "all things" (*pantōn*).[3]

This passage is more dynamic, less timeless, than the opening to John's Gospel. It suggests an unfolding drama: God has spoken before in various ways, but in these last days he has spoken clearly in the Son. Thus the past is gathered

up. Likewise, the Son has been "appointed heir of all things."
Thus the future is anticipated. But lest it be thought—as
many Christians have done—that this future fulfillment is
only for human beings, the "all things" of the future is
squarely rooted in the cosmos: "through whom he made the
universe." (Here "universe" translates the Greek word
aionēs, a cosmological term sometimes linked with cosmos,
but having much more the sense of recurring cycles.)

A third key passage linking Christ to the cosmos is in
the first chapter of Colossians. Again, I use a section of
Paulos Gregorios' translation:

> He, Christ, the Beloved Son, is the manifest presence (icon)
> of the unmanifest God. He is the Elder Brother of all things
> created, for it was by him and in him that all things were
> created, whether here on earth in the sensible world. . . .
> All things were created through him, by him, in him. But he
> himself is before all things; in him they consist and subsist;
> he is the head of the body, the Church. He is the New Begin-
> ning, the Firstborn from the dead; thus he becomes in all
> respects preeminent. For it was (God's) good pleasure that in
> Christ all fullness should dwell; it is through him and in
> him that all things are to be reconciled and reharmonized.
> For he has removed the contradiction and made peace by
> his own blood. So all things in the visible earth and in the
> invisible heaven should dwell together in him. . . .
> That includes you, who were once alienated, enemies
> in your own minds to God's purposes, immersed in evil
> actions; but now you are bodily reconciled in his fleshly
> body which has tasted death. Christ intends to present
> you—holy, spotless, and blameless—in God's presence, if
> you remain firm in the faith, rooted and grounded in him,
> unswerving from the hope of the goods news you have
> heard, the good news declared not only to men and women
> on earth, but to all created beings under heaven. . . .[4]

This is the fullest single passage that deals with the cosmic dimensions of the Gospel. It states even more explicitly
the mystery that in Christ, "all things" (Gk. *panta*) hold
together because "in him they were created." But this pas-

sage goes much further than the other two in describing the link between the Christ of creation and the Christ of the cross. He is to be the one in whom all things are reconciled and brought into harmony. Paul is explicit that it is not just human beings that are thus brought into harmony, but "all things." That reconciliation is linked directly to Jesus' death on the cross. But perhaps the most remarkable thing about this passage is that it reverses the way in which centuries of Western theological discourse have talked about the work of salvation. Today there is an acknowledgment that perhaps all creation is to be reconciled with God—as though other creatures are included grudgingly in a gift intended primarily for human beings. But the wording of Colossians 1:23 implies rather that this gospel is fundamentally for all things, and that humanity has been graciously included: "the good news [is] declared not only to men and women on earth, but to all created things under heaven."

Many other brief passages allude explicitly to the belief that Jesus Christ is Lord of the cosmos, that he is the creating and sustaining energy of the universe as well as its final reconciliation. But the three passages already cited should be sufficient to show that this dimension of the gospel is not at all peripheral. The cosmic concern of salvation is a central theme of the New Testament.

If this is so, why have "all things" except human beings so often been excluded from our understanding of the gospel? Why have those Christian groups most concerned with evangelism, with personal salvation and holy living, often been last to see that the reconciliation between persons and their creator is incomplete if it does not include a reconciliation with the creation from which they are estranged? There is no simple answer. But some light is shed on the question if we reflect on the nature of the central paradox of the gospel: that the Creator God, the Lord of the universe, has become flesh, has entered the human condition, has submitted to the limits of time and place, and has become a living human being along with us.

This paradox is particularly acute when the transcendence and holiness of God is so defended that God's stooping to his creation seems to sully his holiness. One can, for example, see this today in the fierce Islamic defense of the holiness of Allah. The Christian shares this passionate defense of the divine holiness and transcendence (of course, it was a Jewish and Christian theme long before it became the central pillar in Islam). With nothing is the Creator to be confused. Indeed the very shape of the Genesis creation account conveys this divine transcendence. It is often pointed out that many of the things that are worshiped by the surrounding cultures—the sun, moon, sea, four-footed creatures—are described as being made effortlessly by God, in part perhaps as an apologetic argument against those religions. (This is particularly true of the sun, which perhaps explains why in the Genesis account it is not even created until the fourth day.) This temptation to worship the creature rather than the Creator was strong both in the ancient Near Eastern world of the Old Testament and in the syncretistic Mediterranean world of the first century A.D., the human milieu of the New Testament.

God's Immanence in Pre-Christian Judaism

The transcendence of God can never be exaggerated, but it can be understood wrongly as making God's immanent involvement with creation impossible. Something of this exaggeration of transcendence seems to have made God in the intertestamental period seem more and more unreachable. It is interesting to note a yearning for a more accessible God, therefore, in the centuries before the Incarnation.

In response to this yearning for immanence, there arose in those centuries before Christ a whole series of ways of speaking about God's involvement with the world. Some are deeply rooted in the Old Testament revelation. Others are more fanciful.

Many Old Testament passages, for example, use *rûaḥ* ("spirit") when speaking of some aspect of God's involvement with his creation. It is the involvement of God in creation through God's Spirit that gives life. The psalmist expressed this powerfully in Psalm 104:30. After a vivid description of both human and nonhuman creatures, he said:

> When you send your Spirit,
>   they are created,
>   and you renew the face of the earth.[5]

This picture in Psalm 104 of all things being "created" through the Spirit is particularly significant because of the obvious way in which the structure of the Psalm parallels the creation account in Genesis 1. But in Genesis the creation is described as something that is accomplished once-for-all at the beginning. Taken by itself, that account of creation has fueled the picture of God as the transcendent craftsman who makes a perfect work and then withdraws. That portrayal of divine detachment in Genesis 1 is balanced here by a portrayal of divine involvement. Creation is not so much something God did as something God is doing: "He makes springs pour water into the ravines; . . . He waters the mountains. . . . He makes grass grow for the cattle" (Ps. 104:10, 13, 14). And in verse 30 all of this life-giving action of God is centered in the creating Spirit.

Jürgen Moltmann had a great deal to say about the Spirit of God in creation. He agreed that the picture of creation by the Spirit involves a far more intimate connection between Creator and creation than is conveyed in the unbiblical notion of God as "cause" of all things:

> Creating the world is something different from causing it. If the Creator is himself present in his creation by virtue of the Spirit, then his relationship to creation must rather be

viewed as an intricate web of unilateral, reciprocal and many-sided relationships.[6]

Thus, Moltmann saw the presence of God's Spirit in creation as characterized by community and mutuality—God's immanence in creation, as contrasted to God's transcendence over it:

> In this network of relationships, 'making,' 'reserving,' 'maintaining' and 'perfecting' are certainly the great one-sided relationships, but 'indwelling,' 'sympathizing,' 'participating,' 'accompanying,' 'enduring,' 'delighting,' and 'glorifying' are relationships of mutuality which describe a cosmic community of living between God the spirit and all his created beings.[7]

Moltmann also suggested that the indwelling Spirit in creation points to the fact that relationships are more basic than "things" or particles. Creation is "a dynamic web of interconnected processes" bound together by the indwelling Spirit. And though Moltmann reached these conclusions from more bases than that provided by Psalm 104, certainly this great hymn of a creation bound together by the life-giving Spirit suggests that God is deeply involved with his creation.

Similar things could be said of Old Testament uses of "law." Jews of the intertestamental period began to speak of God's closeness to the world almost as a personification of *Torah*, or God's law. Although that personification has little basis in the Old Testament itself, it nevertheless recognizes that the law-giving God is indeed involved in his world. God's law is somehow structured into creation. Thus, in its very being and daily activity, creation can never be far from God, for God' law is part of the very nature of all things.

Christians are used to thinking of law entirely in moral terms, that is, in terms of something that they may or may not do. While that is an important part of biblical

reference to the law, it is by no means all of it. God's law
is in all things. Thus, Psalm 119, that great hymn on the
law, presents the law as central both to human and nonhuman creation:

> Your faithfulness continues through all generations;
>   you established the earth, and it endures.
> Your laws endure to this day,
>   for all things serve you.
> If your law had not been my delight,
>   I would have perished in my affliction.
> I will never forget your precepts.
>
> (Ps. 119:90–93a)

The law is not only the life-giving delight of the psalmist,
but also the enduring faithfulness of the earth itself.

Yet another of the ways in which worshipers of transcendent Yahweh understood God's immanence was
through the concept of wisdom. A significant tradition
developed in Judaism that came very near to personifying
wisdom. The wise sayings of Proverbs are a part of this
tradition, as are Ecclesiastes, Job, and several noncanoni-
cal works, of which the most significant is the Wisdom
of Solomon. But probably the clearest example of this tendency to personify God's wisdom in creation occurs near
the climax of the great invitation which Wisdom utters
in Proverbs 8. Wisdom, personified as female (perhaps as
an apologetic response to the allures of the Egyptian Isis
and other feminine deities), invites "all mankind" to "gain
prudence." She describes in majestic detail the value of
wisdom for human life:

> By me kings reign
>   and rulers make laws that are just;
> by me princes govern,
>   and all nobles who rule on earth.
>
> . . . .
>
> My fruit is better than fine gold;
>   what I yield surpasses choice silver.
>
> (Prov. 8:15, 16, 19)

But the conclusion of this remarkable speech moves (like God's answer to Job) far beyond immediate human concerns and into the heart of creation. First, in terms of that creation, Wisdom asserts her priority: She has been here from the beginning, since before creation:

> The LORD possessed me at the beginning of his work,
>   before his deeds of old;
> I was appointed from eternity,
>   from the beginning, before the world began.
> When there were no oceans, I was given birth,
>   when there were no springs abounding with water;
> before the mountains were settled in place,
>   before the hills, I was given birth
> before he made the earth or its fields,
>   or any of the dust of the world.
>
> (Prov. 8:22–26)

After this declaration that she was present before the beginning of creation, Wisdom goes on to declare that she was present at creation, but she was more than just present—like a master craftsman, she was deeply involved, rejoicing in the work of creation.

> I was there when he set the heavens in place,
>   when he marked out the horizon on the face of the
>   deep,
> when he established the clouds above
>   and fixed securely the fountains of the deep,
> when he gave the sea its boundary
>   so the waters would not overstep his command,
> and when he marked out the foundations of the earth.
>   Then I was the craftsman at his side.
> I was filled with delight day after day,
>   rejoicing always in his presence,
> rejoicing in his whole world
>   and delighting in mankind.
>
> (Prov. 8:27–31)

It would be hard to imagine a picture in greater contrast to the detached Creator that some assume God to be. "Rejoicing," "delighting," and even, as some translations have it, "playing" in creation characterize God's involvement in the cosmos.

My purpose in this discussion of "Spirit," "law," and "wisdom" is to point out that the Old Testament continually walked the line between an affirmation of God's holiness and transcendence and an assertion of his involvement and activity. There was a tendency before the incarnation to divorce God from the cosmos. On the other hand, worshipers of Yahweh, both through human desire and the promptings of the Spirit, arrived at other ways of speaking of God's closeness and participation in what God had made. Thus the way was prepared for the full revelation of the cosmic Christ.

The Atonement of Christ

We have considered some of the texts that speak of the cosmic Christ. Now we must consider how the New Testament teaching of Christ's coming to the whole cosmos fared in the history of the church. We can best summarize this long and complex story by considering the ways in which the church has understood the work of Christ.

Through the course of church history, theologians have attempted to articulate the meaning of Jesus' death. Three major theories of the atonement have resulted from these attempts. Each theory claims to have firm biblical support. While elements of each have always been present in the church, usually only one theory has commanded wide acceptance. Each of the theories stress important truths, but each is incomplete.

For the most part, Western theology for the past 1,000 years has moved between two of these understandings of the atonement.

The Atonement as Satisfaction

One theory of the atonement could be called the "legal," "penal," or "substitutionary" theory. It is by far predominant in orthodox Protestant circles to this day. It is associated particularly with St. Anselm, who in the 11th century A.D. answered the question *Cur Deus Homo?* ("Why the God-man?") by referring to the need of a perfect sacrifice for humanity to satisfy the anger of a just God over sin. This is sometimes called the "satisfaction" theory, and it draws most of its explanation of the atonement from the Old Testament sacrificial system, understood and interpreted in the vocabulary of Roman law. It has dominated both Catholic and Protestant thought until quite recently.

There is abundant New Testament evidence for such an interpretation. The clearest evidence appears in the writings of Paul, particularly in his most systematic exposition, the Epistle to the Romans. After establishing that "all have sinned" (Rom. 3:23), Paul said that they are "justified freely by his grace through the redemption that came by Christ Jesus" (3:24). Then he clearly states that the death of Jesus met the demands for the satisfaction of divine justice:

> God presented him as a sacrifice of atonement, through faith in his blood. He did this to demonstrate his justice, because in his forbearance he had left the sins committed beforehand unpunished—he did it to demonstrate his justice at the present time, so as to be just and the one who justifies those who have faith in Jesus.[8]

But this is only part of the picture, and to explain all of God's action in terms of it would be a mistake.

While Paul knows that the one who is just (God) is also the one who justifies (as in penal, or satisfaction theories of the atonement), it is the action of Jesus as the perfect man that is central here rather than the action of Jesus as the creating and loving God, the cosmic Christ, the Word in whom all things hold together.

The fact that God himself suffered on the cross is not really crucial to the satisfaction theory of the atonement, nor is the fact of the incarnation—that God chose to enter human flesh—seen as anything more than a necessity (since no other perfect man could be found) for the appeasement of God's wrath.

Put another way, the satisfaction theory succeeds in preserving the transcendence of God—he appears always as the implacable judge, beholding from afar the suffering of Christ. Although those who hold this view of the atonement usually do not question the deity of Christ, that divinity is not thought to be the reason for the efficacy of his death. God's immanence is incidental. That it is God himself, the Creator, who suffered in Christ, is not central to this substitutionary idea of the atonement.

The Atonement as Example

Another understanding of the atonement that has been prominent in the West could be called the "exemplarist" or "moral influence" theory of the atonement. Abelard in the 12th century was the first to articulate it, but it did not become prominent until after the enlightenment, and it continues now as a mainstay of "liberal" Christian ethics. It could be called the "exemplarist" theory, for it maintains that in Christ we have the supreme example of how he ought to behave. Christ is the pattern for our lives. Therefore, the change brought by his death is a subjective one, wrought in the mind and will of the person touched by his example.

Put simply, the satisfaction view suggests that the atonement "works" because the death of Jesus changed the mind of God, and the exemplarist view "works" because it changes the minds of human beings. The first view stresses the inability of human beings to save themselves. The second view stresses the necessity of human response to God's action.

As has been suggested, much of the theological battlefield of the last two centuries has taken place between lines drawn by these two understandings of the atonement. The liberal tradition maintains that the moral example of Jesus in his life and death is sufficient to prompt persons to follow him. More conservative theologians, however, with a less optimistic view of human nature, argue that no amount of good examples will make any difference to human beings or God: human righteousness is like dirty clothes, anyway. What matters is that God's righteousness must be satisfied by the punishment of a perfect victim—and only in Jesus was such a perfect victim found.

The differences between these two views will not be resolved here. But for these considerations it is sufficient to point out that neither theory makes the cosmic dimension of Christ's lordship important. In neither theory is it fundamentally important that Jesus is God—that it is our Creator who dies for us. If Jesus' death is important because only a perfect sacrifice will appease the wrath of God, then it is true that God's Son is the only perfect sacrifice. But if a perfect person could be found elsewhere, he or she would do.

Likewise, the force of moral example in the exemplarist view does not come from the fact that it was the Creator himself who hung on the cross. If a perfect person could have been found, he or she too would have provided a sufficient example. So both theories ignore the crucial paradox of our faith, namely, that it was the Creator, the Word who created all things, who suffered on the cross.

Thus neither understanding of the atonement gives much significance to the enormous fact of Christ's cosmic lordship. And since these understandings of the atonement do not stress Christ's involvement with creation apart from humanity, it is not surprising that the ethic

that has developed from those understandings has likewise neglected the human involvement in creation.

The Atonement as Renewal of Creation

For the foundation of an ethic that involves human
beings in creation, it is necessary to return to a more
ancient understanding of the atonement that is rooted in
New Testament cosmic Christology.

This earliest understanding by the church sees the
work of Christ as a "recapitulation" of God's intention
in creation. Christ is the New Adam, restoring the first
Adam and his work. Just as Satan achieved power over
humanity through the sin of the first Adam, he is
defeated through the obedience of the Second Adam. And
in that victory, Jesus reaffirms the task of the first Adam,
inviting persons into renewed fellowship with God, with
each other, and with the earth. Glimpses of this ancient
understanding of salvation as the restoration of creation
are most prominent in the Book of Isaiah[9] and Revelation 21, although it clearly underlies much of the New
Testament.

Irenaeus in the 2d century A.D. was the first to clearly
articulate the recapitulation idea. The following words
capture the flavor of his thought:

> For the Creator of the world is truly the Word of God: and
> this is our Lord, who in the last times was made man,
> existing in this world, and who in an invisible manner con-
> tains all things created, and is inherent in the entire cre-
> ation, since the Word of God governs and arranges all
> things; and therefore He came to His own in a visible man-
> ner, and was made flesh, and hung upon the tree, that He
> might sum up all things in Himself. . . .[10]

Athanasius, likewise, placed at the center of his thought
the fact that our Savior is also our Creator:

We will begin, then, with the creation of the world and with God its Maker, for the first fact that you must grasp is this: the renewal of creation has been wrought by the Self-same Word Who made it in the beginning. There is thus no inconsistency between creation and salvation; for the One Father has employed the same Agent for both works, effecting the salvation of the world through the same Word Who made it at the first.[11]

It is renewal that God works: not only ransom, satisfaction, or example (though it is all of those things). And it is renewal of creation. For the transcendent Creator himself has entered and remade the creation from which he was never far away. As Athanasius put it:

For this purpose, then, the incorporeal and incorruptible and immaterial Word of God entered our world. In one sense, indeed, He was not far from it before, for no part of creation had ever been without Him Who, while ever abiding in union with the Father, yet fills all things that are. But now he entered the world in a new way. . . .[12]

Athanasius is wrestling with the mystery of God's transcendence and immanence. God is the Creator, beyond all worlds; yet God is as well the Logos, upholder of all things. He is immanent in them from the beginning, yet, in the incarnation, he enters the world in a new way. God remakes creation because the Logos is creation's maker, the cosmic Christ.

This understanding of the atonement does the most justice to the full New Testament teaching of Christ's involvement in the cosmos both as Creator and Redeemer (while it does not contradict the others). In it, nothing is exempt from being touched by redemption. In the grand statement of Ephesians 1:10, it is his purpose "to bring all things in heaven and on earth together under one head, even Christ."

Why has our concept of salvation shrunk to include merely the personal? Perhaps the question cannot be answered, but Frederick Dillistone made an intriguing observation:

> The smaller the dimensions of man's world, the more wide-ranging is likely to be his systematic account of reconciliation. As his world expands, so his system seems to contract. When the limits of his universe have vanished into far-off distances, his concentration of concern tends to be focused upon the small-scale world of the isolated inner self. Such a sequence can certainly be seen in the history of theories of the atonement.[13]

Something like the following seems to have happened: as the human understanding of the cosmos became broader, the understanding of salvation became narrower. But it is not clear that the process is necessary, or irreversible. Certainly in Eastern Orthodox churches today there is a robust understanding of the "divinization" of all creation, and of the human destiny to stand as a kind of mediator between God and all the rest of creation. Thus, from this context come the powerful words from the late Vladimir Lossky, an Orthodox theologian:

> In his way to union with God, man in no way leaves creatures aside, but gathers together in his love the whole cosmos disordered by sin, that it may at last be transfigured by grace.[14]

To stand thus in such a redemptive role toward creation is what being called into sonship with the cosmic Christ means. It is not that we are all Christs. Here we must differ strenuously with some of the statements of Matthew Fox, who implies that we are all Christs and have simply to discover it. In contrast, the New Testament teaches that Christ graciously enables us to share both in God's immanence and transcendence. Through Christ, we represent God toward creation.

Creation and the Suffering of God

God sharing God's power with us is an enormous danger, whether in our secular deification of humanity, or in our various Christian confidences that we are doing God's will. The temptation to say, "I am God," is as ancient as Adam, and is rightly seen as lying at the heart of many of our environmental problems. Accordingly, it is when we think that we have divine power over the rest of creation that we are likely to crush it, whether that devastation be as dramatic as the nuclear disaster at Chernobyl, or as trivial as household garbage.

Those who say biblical teaching about human salvation encourages them to think that they are like God miss one enormously important truth, a truth that makes it possible for Christians to speak of following the cosmic Christ without advocating their transformation into some sort of Promethean supermen. That truth lies at the center of Christian faith: the cost of creation is the suffering of God.

We humans have enormous creative powers, and we learn each year to exercise them more effectively. That is not inappropriate for those made in God's image. But when we exercise them for our own glorification, we are not following the cosmic Christ of the New Testament. He is the Creator, but he is also "the lamb slain before the foundation of the world." To follow him—in stewardship, in earthkeeping—is also to open oneself up to death. As Bonhoeffer said, "When Christ calls a man, he bids him come and die."[15]

The words of Charles Williams are eloquent here:

He was stretched, he was bled, he was nailed. He was thrust into, but not a bone of Him was broken. The dead wood drenched with the blood and the dead body shedding blood have an awful likeness; the frame is doubly saved. It was the Cross which sustained Him, but He also sustained the Cross. He had, through the years, exactly preserved the growth of the thorn and of the wood, and had indued with energy the making of the nails and the sharpening of the spear; say through the centuries He had maintained vegetable and mineral in the earth for this. His providence overwatched it to no other end, as it over-watches so many instruments and intentions of cruelty then and now. The Cross therefore is the express image of His will.[16]

A Personal Postscript

In one room of my Galiano Island house hangs a large three-panel painting by Linsey Farrell, an Australian painter who, based on his sensitive visual explorations of the Australian landscape, won an award from the Queens-land government to go abroad to paint. He came to Regent College (where I teach) in part to experience our vast, rich network of interrelated life of western Canada, which seems to dwarf the human presence. One way to respond is the pioneer's way: to chop it down, dig it up, pave it over; reduce it as rapidly as possible to a safely human world. Is that the Christian way? Linsey's paintings have tried to ask that question.

The painting in our house hangs in a light-filled room that looks down into Retreat Cove and over to tree-cov-ered Retreat Island, a few hundred yards off shore. Seals, otters, herons, loons, cormorants, gulls, and eagles are reg-ular citizens of the place. The left panel of Linsey's paint-ing portrays the island as it is in its setting, ringed by sea and mountains. The right-hand panel shows a rock-ringed lake (the subject of several of Linsey's earlier British Columbia paintings), one of the sources of a mountain river that flows into the sea near us. A line of hills and mountains forms the skyline of all three panels of the painting, reaching from above the island on the left to above the lake on the right. On the center panel is another form: It is Retreat Island clear-cut and burned (as is much of our larger island now), the dead trees and logging debris forming a thorn-like crown.

And then—it catches some with almost a physical shock—one sees that the hills forming the skyline of the painting are also the shoulders of a strong man hanging from his arms, and that the central panel is indeed a crown of thorns. The figure of the crucified Christ encompasses the painting, his arms enclosing the treed island on the left, and the lake of clear water on the right, which is also an empty tomb. And in the center, the wounds inflicted on the island by thoughtless human activity are also inflicted on the One whose arms uphold the hills. The painting challenges nearly everyone who sees it. Of the sophisticated pagan environmentalists it asks, Are you correct in dismissing the Christian story as irrelevant to your concern for the earth? And of Christians it asks, Did Jesus die just for you? Or did he die for the whole creation? I think there is little doubt of the answer.

2

Christ as the Second Adam

Ronald Manahan

Adam himself lies now scattered on the whole surface of the earth. Formerly concentrated in one place, he has fallen; having been broken to pieces, as it were, he has filled the universe with his debris. However, God's mercy has gathered together from everywhere his fragments and by fusing them in the fire of his charity, has reconstituted their broken unity.

St. Augustine's words from *The City of God* appropriately capture the Christian's human condition: in the midst of debris, living with hope in the good mercy of God. The belief is that God is in the process of putting together the broken pieces, reconstituting the unity God desires. God's stewards seek that wholeness which characterizes God's kingdom. Their work, though sometimes halting, is periodically enlivened by a fresh opportunity to discern the mind of God as best they can in the condi-

tion of fallenness. Each time they do, they gain a somewhat clearer vision of the nature and scope of the work
of stewards.

A suspicion that disheartens these efforts is that the
very portion of Scripture on which the church builds so
much of its teaching, namely, the New Testament, gives
little or no instruction on how to act as stewards. Is this
really the situation? This essay will argue that the central message of the New Testament presents a pervasive
stewardship calling to all who are redeemed.

Reading Scripture as a Whole

While the text of the Old Testament has furnished followers of Christ an abundance of materials giving guidance to their care of creation, many believe that the New
Testament remains nearly silent on the issue. For certain
sectors of the Christian church, this seeming silence has
provided opportunity to downplay the importance of activity. Reasons for thinking of stewardship as being driven
primarily by the Old Testament are many, to be sure.
None, however, is more profound in its damaging impact
than the continued dichotomizing of the Old Testament
and the New Testament texts as though they were separate canons, as though the one does not inform the other.
This separation has occasioned an unfortunate approach to
both testaments, especially the New. Through this bifur-
cation within the canon, those linkages between the two
testaments have been severed. These links would broaden
canonical insight, sensitize biblical methodology, and
make for better readers of the canon. They would help
envision so grand an *inclusio* as the one in Genesis 1–3
and Revelation 20–22, one clearly pointing to the unity
of the testaments. In this *inclusio* the damaged beginning
is restored at the end. The garden has become the city,
but the city is reminiscent of the garden. On the other
hand, familiarity with the garden helps one identify the

city. There seems to be a conscious linking of the beginning and end of the whole canon.

Commitment to Scripture through this holistic approach means that every particular text must be read as having an organic connectedness to the whole of the canon. No passage is read in isolation. Nor is any book. Nor is either testament. Viewing Scripture in this way is an especially appropriate approach when reading certain passages that may give very helpful stewardship guidance. For in these passages the biblical authors present sweeping remarks in which both old and new elements are brought together in a powerful interpretive complex.

Few are more expansive than the first Adam-last (second) Adam passages. When read in their canonical setting, they become fruitful New Testament guides for practice.

The Analogy of Adam and Christ

On two clear occasions, the New Testament compares Adam and Christ in such a way that Christ is said to undo the damage caused by Adam. As 1 Corinthians 15:21–22 succinctly puts it: "For since death came through a man, the resurrection of the dead comes also through a man. For as in Adam all die, so in Christ all will be made alive." Romans 5:12–21 gives an extended first Adam-last Adam presentation. D. E. H. Whitely correctly noted that "many of St. Paul's fundamental doctrines can be properly understood only if we realize that he took for granted the presupposition of human solidarity."[1] The apostle could do this precisely because of his religious background. In Hebrew culture (in fact throughout the ancient Near East), the solidaristic relationship played a dominant role. The idea may be variously expressed: "solidarity," "corporate personality," "extended personality," or the like. Whatever the designation, the idea as it was expressed years ago by Robinson is that the whole group—including its past, present, and future members, might function as a single individual through any one of those members conceived as representative of it. Because it was not confined to the living, but included the dead and the unborn, the group could be conceived as living for ever.[2]

The fluidity of the concept would allow for one to represent the entire group, or the group to sum up all the individuals.

Assuming this solidaristic concept, Paul is able to see both Adam and Christ as representatives. Adam's personal destiny is made determinative for their (i.e., all who die) personal destinies. Likewise, Christ's destiny is determinative for many, also.[3] This analogy between the first Adam and the last Adam (Christ) is spelled out in Romans 5:12–21. Several observations concerning this passage are relevant to a Christian understanding of stewardship. The first observation concerns the very organization of the passage. Verse 12 records the protasis[4] of an incomplete sentence. C. C. Caragounis correctly suggested that the entire sentence, had it been given in verse 12, might have read like this: "Therefore, as by one man sin entered the world and death (entered the world) through sin, so also justification came into the world through one and life through justification."[5] However, the thought in verse 12 is incomplete and is followed by a digression (occasioned by the mention of death) in 5:13–14. In fact, the apodosis[6] is not presented until 5:18b.

Verses 15–17 provide Paul an opportunity to question the readers. Verses 15a and 16a may be read as questions.[7] The questions (expecting a yes answer) are intended to allow the readers to agree that Christ's work avails for those he represents, a process similar to that by which Adam's work avails for those he represents.[8] The structure of the text can be outlined as in figure 2.1.

Fig. 2.1

The Structure of Romans 5:12–19

5:12, **protasis**, "Therefore, just as sin entered the world . . ."
   5:13–14c, Digression concerning death
   5:15–17, Two questions leading to assent of readers:
      Question One: 5:15a, "But does not the free gift operate
      just like the trespass did?"
      5:15b, *Answer*, "For if the many died by . . ."
      Question Two: 5:16a, "And is not the free gift transmit-
      ted in the same way as sin was transmitted by the one
      who sinned?"
      5:16b, Explanatory *gar* ("for") statement to emphasize
      the one versus the many
      5:17, *Answer*, "For if, by the trespass of . . ."
   5:18a, repeats protasis of 5:12
5:18b, **apodosis**, ". . . so also the result of one act of . . ."
5:19, repeats the gist of 5:12–18, putting together the protasis
of 5:12 and the apodosis of 5:18b

In this understanding of the passage the questions of
5:15–17 play a key role. They are employed to overcome a
potential problem. The readers accept the fact that Adam's
sin produces consequences of sin and death for all. This
does not mean, however, that they will necessarily accept
the dogma that Christ's work has the positive effects
claimed by the apostle. Paul presents the questions to
encourage the readers to count as fact the effects of the
work of both the first and last Adam. Through this means,
the apostle has drawn the analogy between Adam and
Christ and sees them as representatives of their respective groups.

Cosmic Implications of the Work
of the Two Adams

A further observation about the Romans 5 passage is
also helpful. Should the work of the two Adams be under-

stood as cosmic? In some circles Romans 5 and other such passages are read only as having personal salvific implications. In this way the impact of the work of the two representatives—though including all humanity—is seen in somewhat narrow terms. Personal condemnation and salvation have no cosmic connections. While the personal is certainly here, it is never divorced from the cosmic. As the work of the first Adam had cosmic effects, so does the work of the last Adam. Several factors point to this reality.

It must be remembered that Paul's thinking was shaped by his Hebrew background. When he compared Adam and Christ, he certainly thought of Adam and the consequences of his work in terms of the Hebrew Scriptures. So Christ is compared with Adam as the latter was understood in these terms.

Reviewing the Old Testament's presentation of Adam highlights several points of interest. One is Adam's interconnectedness with the rest of created reality. Adam is presented as existing within a threefold relationship: God, the world (as Israel understood it), and others.[9] Genesis 1:26–28 presents a clear summary of this. Human beings are made in God's "image" (Heb. *ṣelem*) and "likeness" (Heb. *dĕmût*). Both of these terms are very concrete and can be used to refer to physical representations.[10] This assertion of physical correspondence with God must be understood in this way: "man even in his corporeality has a correspondence, likeness, to God."[11] The Hebrews conceived of human beings holistically, so it is not surprising that persons in their *totality* should be viewed as corresponding to God.

Individuals also stand in relationship to others. This reality is presented in the observation that God created persons male and female and "blessed them and said to them, 'Be fruitful and increase in number; fill the earth. . . .'"[12] Here, and in Genesis 2:24, social ordering is implied. Ever-increasing levels of social complexity are suggested by these early remarks in Genesis. Persons are in community with others from the beginning; the quality of the relationship varies; the fact of it, however, is constant.[13]

According to Genesis 1:26–28, human beings also stand in relationship to the rest of the world, roughly signified by the Greek word *kosmos*. This relationship is described by the words "rule" (Heb. *rādâ*) and "subdue" (*kābaŝ*). These are certainly forceful terms, but neither by itself necessarily pictures harshness. This element must be supplied by the context.[14] These terms are ones of action, *doing* as a consequence of what humans are (image-bearers). The action is formative and shaping, but always as a consequence of what humans are.[15]

This threefold relationship is lived out within an ethical understanding common to the ancient Near East, including portions of the Old Testament itself.[16] The view among these ancients seems to have been that all persons saw themselves as standing within a spectrum of beings. There was always someone just above and someone just beneath. To the one above, a person owed obedience; to the one beneath, beneficence. This simple arrangement provided an ethical framework for decision making.

This insight into an individual's threefold relationship can be graphed as a hierarchical ethical arrangement, as in figure 2.2.

Fig. 2.2

The Individual's Threefold Relationship

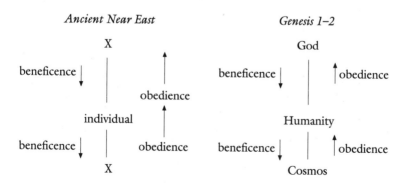

This ethical framework is found repeatedly among king-ship materials in the ancient Near East.[17] The king stands between the gods and the kingdom in its fullest sense. As the king obeys the gods, the gods respond with benefi-cence toward the kingdom. Of course, the opposite is also true. Disobedience to the gods brings their curse on the kingdom. There are excellent examples of this pivotal role played by the king in the Old Testament.[18] In this light it is especially noteworthy that the vocabulary of Genesis 1:26–28 is profoundly royal in nature. A second point to note is that disobedience and cursing go hand in hand just as do obedience and beneficence. The point is that dis-ruption of one relationship brings ruination in other rela-tionships. A very good example of this is in Psalm 14 where the fool, who says "There is no God" (Ps. 14:1), is the very one who abuses the poor!

In Genesis 2 and 3 two presentations are given—one positive and one negative—of how this ethical structur-ing worked out for the first Adam. Genesis 2 pictures Adam in the garden. In this setting his relationships were harmonious and complete; he had an open, obedient rela-tionship with God, his relationship with Eve was harmo-nious, and he was given the task of a caring guardianship (stewardship) with respect to the cosmos. This is a pic-ture of how it ought to be. In fact, the Hebrew term šālôm, "well-being," describes it. Obedience and beneficence worked together. This becomes the stuff of which future longings for an ideal king in Israel are made.[19] But Genesis 3 gives a negative picture, one of disobedience and cursing. When Adam fell, the threefold relationship unraveled. He disobeyed God (Gen. 3:1–7) and experienced distance from him (3:8–10). The harmony with Eve was undone (3:11–16). The caring stewardship of the cosmos turned to cursing and estrangement (3:17–19). Human beings became homeless, dismissed from the garden (3:23–24). Genesis 3 soberly depicts disobedience leading to cursing. The beneficence with which persons were to carry out stewardship of the earth was gone.

Applying Old Testament Ideas to the New

From the beginning, the Scriptures present the first Adam's disobedience as having very broad implications; his relationship with God impacted all other essential relationships. Adam's sin was not simply personal. It was that, to be sure. But it was much more far-reaching, including how he related to others and to the cosmos. This is why, to the Hebrew way of thinking, obeying God includes caring, beneficent relationships with others and with the cosmos. Disobedience toward God opens one to poor, uncaring, abusive relationships with others and the cosmos. The true kingdom of God is one of harmony and care; the opposite is a kingdom of cursing and abuse.

For the apostle Paul, all of the above could not help but have profound implications, especially when he drew the analogy between Christ and Adam. Paul saw that the effect of the obedience of Christ was as broad as the effect of the disobedience of Adam. That, it appears, was the apostle's framework for comparing the first and last Adam. When Paul thought of Adam, he thought of him in the context of the Hebrew world. This is what makes the comparison of the first and last Adam so telling, so full of meaning. The work of Christ is not only personal but cosmic. It is designed for the redemption of persons *and* relationships with others and the cosmos. The beneficence of these good relationships comes through the One who was fully obedient to his Father, even to the point of experiencing the agony of the cross. Those who stand in the obedience of Christ have the most profound reason for practicing caring relationships and stewardship. The New Testament is vocal, not silent, on the matter of stewardship.

In Romans 5 the apostle presented the last Adam as undoing the damaging effects of the first Adam. All that the first Adam wrecks, the last Adam restores. As Steele and Thomas pointed out, the passage refers to "two men, two acts, two results."[20] In the light of the Old Testament, these sets of two might be viewed as in figure 2.3.

Fig. 2.3

The Two Adams

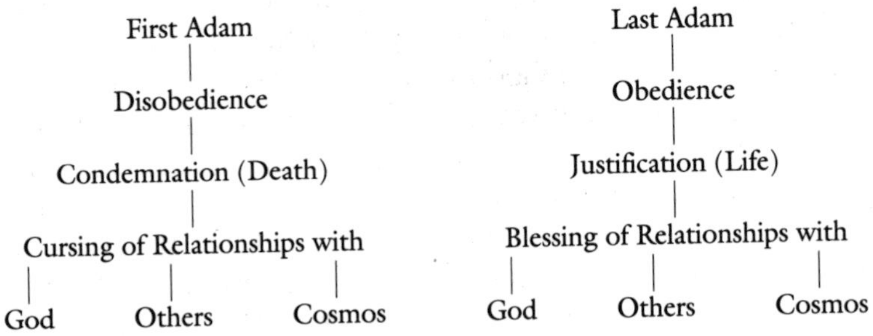

First Adam	Last Adam
Disobedience	Obedience
Condemnation (Death)	Justification (Life)
Cursing of Relationships with	Blessing of Relationships with
God Others Cosmos	God Others Cosmos

What the last Adam brought was "the gift of righteousness,"[21] an expression that may well be freighted with the broad implications of righteousness in the Old Testament. The meaning of this concept is illustrated in Psalm 72, a song exploring the role a future king of Israel might play. Here "righteousness" almost has the meaning "destined," "legitimate," or "right."[22] In fact, the word is paired with "prosperity" (Heb. *šālôm*), a term meaning "well-being," in Psalm 72:2–3. These Hebrew connotations, with which Paul was undoubtedly familiar, give guidance for thinking about the broad implications of other remarks in Romans 5:

5:16b	*brought* justification
5:18b	justification that brings life
5:19b	will be made righteous
5:21b	through righteousness

Paul, assuming the sacred writings of his people, saw the work of Christ as aimed at cosmic well-being, *šālôm*, a fullness of life that enriches its totality. The first Adam brought cursing in all of its fullness. But from this Paul was able to construct an analogy between Adam and Christ. The analogy (or typology) builds upon a historical correspondence: both Adam and Christ are representatives.[23] In the movement of the analogy from Adam to Christ there is an escalation, an upward sweep. The culmination of this sweep is that, whereas Adam begets death, Christ begets life through the startling event of the resurrection.[24] The last enemy, death, is destroyed. Now there is the possibility for "well-being" and "life." So the apostle understood the reach of Christ's work as extending everywhere.[25]

An Encouragement

In the light of the suggestions of this study, the work of the last Adam is as broad as the reach of the damage of the first Adam. The work of Christ impacts relationships with God, others, and the cosmos. Those who follow Christ dare not narrow the application of Christ's work, thereby ignoring its cosmic dimensions. The followers of the last Adam should be foremost among those vitally interested in the cosmos. Rather than being silent on stewardship, the New Testament encourages Christians to see the work of the last Adam as the reconciliation of all relationships. By obeying the last Adam, Christians have the potential for practicing true beneficence toward the cosmos. One day Christ will show fully the meaning of a stewardship driven by true and total loyalty to the Father.[26]

If the Christian's calling is to live out Christ's salvation, it must also be one of stewardship. The calling is one of obedience *and* beneficence. But what does this mean in more specific terms? This calling means that the vertical relationship with God should never be divorced from horizontal relationships with others and the cosmos. Being a follower of God requires engaging all of these relationships to God's glory. Redemption is redemption of the soul, of relationships with others, and the cosmos. The call of Christ, therefore, ties together caring for others and caring for earth, an "ecojustice," so to speak. Although having a different understanding of Christianity than the one guiding this study, William Gibson put the matter in helpful terms:

> Ecojustice involves a bifocal vision of economic and environmental justice. It is not that we want the well-being of humankind and the well-being of nature, as if these represented two separate sets of concerns; rather we can't have one without the other.[27]

Gibson touched on a very important point, one that grows naturally from this study. The threefold relationship of persons does not represent three separate concerns; rather, to have any one of them, one must also have the other two. This is the issue that the redeeming activity of Christ, the last Adam, addressed.

So the Christian calling is broad and inclusive. It may be summed up as the redeemed practice of total obedience and beneficence, tracing ever more faithfully the steps of Christ who perfectly did both. And as encouragement, God has presented to us a description of how God made the earth and how God will re-make it. These pictures give us a knowledge of God's goals, and that of all Christians.

3

Christ's Resurrection

and the Creation's Vindication

Raymond C. Van Leeuwen

From time to time in the history of the Christian church, believers proclaim their intention to be "New Testament Christians." This approach to the New Testament often works in this manner: If you are not sure how to "do the right thing," you ask what the New Testament has to say on the subject. The idea is that if you do literally what the New Testament says, you will be blameless in a sinful world, as will the church of God. So you look for relevant New Testament "proof texts." This sort of thinking no doubt proceeds from good intentions, but is unsatisfactory in the end. While provisionally helpful, it is too limiting in the quest to be biblical Christians in God's creation. There are sev-

eral reasons for this, some of which are worth considering at the outset.

First, it is no longer the first century A.D. Without much
thought, one can see that the world has changed since the
days Jesus walked in sandals and a robe. There are no New
Testament texts directly offering guidance and commentary on nuclear war and waste, genetic engineering, wetlands, ozone depletion, rain forest burning, garbage dis-
posal, or MTV. Nowhere in the New Testament will one
find the word or even the concept of "environment" in
its modern sense. How then can the New Testament
speak to these pressing concerns that face all thoughtful
human beings? Many have concluded that it has nothing
to say and that Christians should get on with the business of saving souls out of a seemingly hostile world. They
counsel others not to worry about strip mining or similar environmental problems. For instance, President Rea-
gan's former Secretary of the Interior, James Watt, was
forced to resign largely because of his callous attitude concerning violence to the creation. He is a New Testament
Christian, but unfortunately he believed that Christ's
imminent return made stewardship of the earth unnec-
essary.[1]

Second, those who desire to be New Testament Christians often forget that the Old Testament was the only
written Word of God for the apostolic church. In fact when
Paul wrote, "All Scripture is God-breathed and is useful
for teaching, rebuking, correcting and training in righteousness, so that the man of God may be thoroughly
equipped for every good work,"[2] he was speaking of the
Old Testament. New Testament scholars know that the
New Testament is filled with quotations from and allu-
sions to Old Testament texts and principles. But this
knowledge often does not function in the life of God's
people. When the New Testament is cut off from its Old
Testament roots, it may be misread in terms of contemporary cultural prejudices and blinders. Not only laypeople, but even great scholars make this mistake.

The ancient model for such a misreading is provided by the heretic Marcion (excommunicated in A.D. 144). Marcion rejected the Old Testament and its Creator God as alien to the God and Father of Jesus Christ. The New Testament God

> was wholly other than the God who could be known either from the creation or from Old Testament revelation. . . . Marcion separated his authentic Christ from the political Messiah of the Jews by "a great and absolute difference." This authentic Christ could not have assumed a material body that participated in the created world, for such a body would have been "stuffed with excrement." A material body and a physical birth . . . were unworthy of the true Christ.[3]

Basic to Marcion's rejection of the Old Testament was a Greek-Gnostic hatred of the created order. "The natural world was made up of 'beggarly elements,' among which Marcion especially included reptiles and insects. Particularly repulsive to him was the 'uncleanness' of sex and childbirth, none of which could have anything to do with the salvation of man."[4] Thus Marcion not only rejected the Old Testament, he edited the New Testament, cutting out parts he found offensive, and reinterpreted key doctrines. "The resurrection of the body . . . had to be changed into 'the salvation of the soul.'"[5] Instead of hoping for a "new creation," a "new heavens and a new earth in which righteousness dwells,"[6] Marcion rejected the creation and saw salvation as escape from creation, escape from the body.

Marcion's Gnostic hatred of creation is relevant to this conversation because his (less consistent) followers still exist today. They do not rewrite the New Testament, but they do ignore its Old Testament foundations and suppress its setting in God's creation. And in our modern Western culture at large, the idea of nature as an enemy to be subjugated—in Francis Bacon's image, "put on the rack"[7] by our technology and exploited for our profit—is merely a secular form of ancient Gnosticism. It is the rejection of God's good order for creation. Ultimately, it is the cultural, communal denial of reality.

Third, connected with the problem of severing the New Testament from the Old is the danger of adopting a proof-text mentality toward the New Testament. The New Testament is a small book with an infinitely important but very limited agenda: to proclaim the gospel of God's grace revealed in the life, death, and resurrection of Jesus Christ; to teach and guide the infant church of Christ, newborn at Pentecost, in light of the gospel; and to point to the final renewal of all things.[8] In the light of this limited agenda, the danger is that it will be mistakenly believed that the New Testament has nothing to say about matters that it does not mention explicitly or elaborate thematically. This approach opens up Christians to the temptation to limit the Good News and claims of Christ to such things as personal morality, piety, and "soul-winning." It seems to allow individuals, rather than Christ, to set the agenda for their lives. Thus most of their affairs, most of the time—in culture and creation—are removed from the claim of Christ. As the godless proverb puts it, "Business is business." The foregoing approaches risk limiting the all-encompassing scope of God's Word and Christ's lordship. They permit the reading of the New Testament with cultural presuppositions alien to the spirit of the New Testament. Thus, the bulk of life is removed from the governing and renewing power of the Gospel.

What is needed is a reading of the New Testament that takes seriously its fundamental theological structures and principles. Such a reading, guided and empowered by the Spirit, should lead to a communal life of praise and obedient service in every area of life. It is empowered by that self-same Spirit, in every area of life, in every nook and cranny of God's world. The mind of Christ must be discerned, as must the underlying principles and presuppositions which undergird the teaching and preaching of the New Testament. When these fundamental structures and principles are discerned and worked out in terms of their "implications" for life in the world, Christians will be astounded at the scope of God's majestic rule and of their task in this present age.

The Vindication of Creation's Goodness

The focus of this essay is Christ's resurrection as the vindication of creation.[9] In this regard, the apostle Paul's proclamation of the resurrection is a main resource. This is not to minimize the cross that preceded the resurrection. Without the atonement—the shedding of blood for sin—there is no resurrection and no redemption. Nothing is more central to Paul's preaching than the crucifixion of Jesus.[10] But it is the resurrection that "demonstrates" the final triumph of Christ's action on the cross. Thus, the focus here lies on the resurrection. If Christ in his death wiped out evil and death, in his resurrection he vindicated the goodness of creation, its renewal and transformation into a new creation.[11] A clue may be taken from Oliver O'Donovan's profound book, *Resurrection and Moral Order*. He wrote:

> We are driven to concentrate on the resurrection as our starting-point because it tells us of God's vindication of his creation, and so of our created life. . . .

> The meaning of the resurrection, as Saint Paul presents it, is that it is God's final and decisive word on the life of his creature, Adam. . . . It might have been possible, we could say, before Christ rose from the dead, for someone to wonder whether creation was a lost cause. If the creature consistently acted to uncreate itself, and with itself to uncreate the rest of creation, did this not mean that God's handiwork was flawed beyond hope of repair? It might have been possible before Christ rose from the dead to

answer in good faith, Yes. Before God raised Jesus from the dead, the hope that we call 'gnostic,' the hope for redemption *from* creation rather than for the redemption *of* creation, might have appeared to be the only possible hope. 'But in fact Christ has been raised from the dead . . .' (15:20). That fact rules out those other possibilities, for in the second Adam the first is rescued. The deviance of his will, its fateful leaning towards death, has not been allowed to uncreate what God created.[12]

The great hymn in Colossians 1:15–20 is the clearest comprehensive statement of this theme. It is foundational for all that follows:

[Christ] is the image of the invisible God, the firstborn over all creation. For by him all things were created: things in heaven and on earth, visible and invisible, . . . all things were created by him and for him. He is before all things, and in him all things hold together. And he is the head of the body, the church; he is the beginning and *the firstborn from among the dead* [italics added], so that in everything he might have the supremacy. For God was pleased to have all his fullness dwell in him, and through him to reconcile to himself all things, whether things on earth or things in heaven, by making peace through his blood, shed on the cross.[13]

First, Christ created all things and redeems all things. Paul emphasized the cosmic scope of Christ's rule and redemption in every possible way.[14] Second, Paul here firmly connected creation, atonement, resurrection, and redemption of the cosmos. Third, this passage stands against every sinful Christian attempt to divide reality into secular and sacred realms. All of reality is Christ's good creation, all of reality is redeemed by him; therefore, all of reality is the responsibility of God's people. Since the church is now Christ's body, his visible presence in this world, it is the church's job to continue the reconciling, cosmic work of Christ until he comes again. This point will become clearer presently in considering 2 Corinthians 5.

Resurrection Righteousness and Creation

In Romans 4:13 Paul establishes the continuity of Christian faith with the creation faith of Abraham: "It was not through law that Abraham and his offspring received the promise that he would be heir of the world, but through the righteousness that comes by faith."[15] The extraordinary implication is that believers are destined to inherit the world. *This* is the fullness of our inheritance in the age to come. The creation theme continues in verse 17 wherein Paul reminds Christians that Abraham believed in the God "who gives life to the dead and calls things that are not as though they were." Here resurrection and creation are parallel realities. The chapter concludes with what might be considered the statement of the theme here. Faith is reckoned as righteousness "for us who believe in him who raised Jesus our Lord from the dead. He was delivered over to death for our sins and was raised to life for our justification."[16]

Now orthodox systematic theology usually associates righteousness and justification with Christ's shed blood on the cross.[17] There Christ's death substituted for our death and so we regained "peace with God"[18] and righteousness. But here it is most curious that Christ was raised for our justification and righteousness. What could Paul mean by this unusual saying? Apparently cross and resurrection work as a unity in making sinners righteous, but what precise role does resurrection play?

Resurrection and righteousness go together because in Christ's resurrection we see the first fruits of a new creation in which all things have been made *right* by atonement. In resurrection, the good creation has reached the beginning of its final glory. Thus the resurrection is the vindication of God's righteousness. It is the first irrefutable evidence of a new humanity,[19] of a new creation which finds its rightness and health in Christ. Christ is the second Adam, the "new self"[20] come to glorious perfection. He is the new "image of God"[21] who provides the model for our re-creation "in true righteousness and holiness."[22] The point for the present environmental concern is that the same Spirit who raised Christ from the dead is now at work in human beings so that they "may live a new life."[23] Since we "have been brought from death to life," our bodies already in this age are "instruments of righteousness."[24] "And if the Spirit of him who raised Jesus from the dead is living in you, he who raised Christ from the dead will also give life to your mortal bodies through his Spirit, who lives in you."[25] This is all to say that the righteousness of God, given to us freely in Christ, now becomes an active spiritual power,[26] a force for good deeds in a creation that still groans awaiting its full and final redemption.[27]

But what precisely is this righteousness which the new life is to manifest in this present world? Paul sends us back to the Old Testament law in its positive sense as a guide to life in the world:

> . . . the law of the Spirit of life set me free from the law of sin and death. . . . in order that the righteous requirements of the law might be fully met in us, who do not live according to the sinful nature but according to the Spirit.[28]

The "righteous requirement of the law" is nothing less than a life lived in harmony with the Creator and the creation. As in the Old Testament, so also in the New, righteousness cannot be understood apart from God's creation order. An extensive exegetical demonstration of this point cannot be made in the confines of this essay, but it is well established in a growing body of scholarship.[29] As was shown in Romans 4, New Testament righteousness is rooted in the creation faith of the Old Testament. This implies that the practical (which springs from the forensic) righteousness of Christians is simply a life in harmony with the Creator and the creation. Righteousness might be defined as *the state of being at peace with the Creator and in a right relation with the creation, including our fellow humans*.[30] The New Testament scholar Peter Stuhlmacher defined this aspect of Paul's doctrine of justification/righteousness as follows:

> [F]or him [Paul] justification means an ontic transformation; concretely it means being placed once again in the original situation of existing in the image of God, in harmony with the creation.[31]

That justified situation means that in Christ we are restored to Adam's position of steward of the earth on behalf of the Creator.[32] Because we share in Christ's resurrection righteousness, we are responsible for the care of the creation.

The Transformation of This World

But some may say, with James Watt, that this world is passing away. Indeed the New Testament seems to say as much in several places.[33] But what precisely does this mean? According to some people who base their view partly on a mistaken understanding of 2 Peter 3:10,[34] this world will be utterly destroyed by fire; there will be a radical break between this world and the next, so that this one does not much matter. Here again we see a Gnostic worldview that is actually alien to the New Testament.

A close look at a neglected section of Paul's great passage on the resurrection shows that this world retains its importance or "splendor" both in its own right and as the "seed" of the world to come. To change the image, this world will not be destroyed but purified and transformed, even as Christ's resurrected body has been transformed and our mortal bodies will be changed. The reference here is to 1 Corinthians 15:35–44:

> But someone may ask, 'How are the dead raised? With what kind of body will they come?' How foolish! What you sow does not come to life unless it dies. When you sow, you do not plant the body that will be, but just a seed, perhaps of wheat or of something else. But God gives it a body as he has determined, and to each kind of seed he gives its own body. All flesh is not the same: Men have one kind of flesh, animals have another, birds another and fish another. There are also heavenly bodies and there are earthly bodies; but the splendor of the heavenly bodies is one kind, and the splendor of the earthly bodies is another. The sun has one kind of splendor, the moon another and the stars another; and star differs from star in splendor.
>
> So will it be with the resurrection of the dead. The body that is sown is perishable, it is raised imperishable; it is sown in dishonor, it is raised in glory; it is sown in weakness, it is raised in power; it is sown a natural[35] body, it is raised a spiritual body.

Paul reserves the phrase "How foolish!" for the person who does not think "creationally" about the world to come. As Christoph Burchard has pointed out, Paul's argument here is based on the creaturely kinds of Genesis 1 and is a form of Old Testament "experiential wisdom."[36] Paul sets thinking about the resurrection firmly within the context of the entire creation. We have bodies of cosmic stuff in this world, and we will have them in the next. Therefore, with our bodies comes the whole panoply of creatures, from plants to animals to the heavenly bodies. Paul parades before us the creatures of Genesis 1, "each according to its kind." He points to the sun, moon, and varied stars. Each creature, even in the present age, has its own goodness and value, or as Paul puts it, its proper "splendor" (doxa).[37] In the glory of earthly things we see reflected the glory of God, "who gives life to everything . . . who richly provides us with everything for our enjoyment."[38]

Moreover, Paul shows great concern for respecting the nature or "kind" of each creature.[39] In his analogy of the resurrection, it is the "kind" of seed that is sown that determines the "kind of body" that "come[s] to life."[40] There is both continuity and change between this world and the next. Moreover, the nature of things in this age, in a certain sense, determines the nature of things in the next. Perhaps the connection is similar to the transformation of a pupa into a butterfly. While the point cannot be developed here, what people do in this world does determine their "splendor" and "reward" in the world to come.[41] "For we must all appear before the judgment seat of Christ, that each one may receive what is due him for the things done while in the body, whether good or bad."[42]

Righteousness and salvation in the New Testament certainly begin with people but are not limited to them. They extend to all of creation. The reason, according to Steck, is that

> the transformation of a world of Creation distorted by people begins with the believing acceptance of the gospel by people; even though God brings this about for the salvation of the nonhuman world of Creation too, as Romans 8 shows particularly. By directing the saving event mainly toward people, before all other created things, the New Testament is reflecting what the Old had already grasped when it saw man as having a particular position and responsibility for the whole world of creation.[43]

The cosmic implications of Christ's death and resurrection are also made clear in the famous passage on reconciliation in 2 Corinthians 5. Through the atoning death and life-giving resurrection of Christ,[44] Christians are clothed with the new life of their risen Lord;[45] Paul says they are "in Christ." And "if anyone is in Christ, he is a new creation; the old has gone, the new has come! All this is from God, who reconciled us to himself through Christ and gave us the ministry of reconciliation: that God was reconciling the world to himself in Christ. . . ."[46] The final renewal of all things has begun already in this age, in Christ and those who are his new creation. But this new creation is by no means a merely human phenomenon that leaves creation as a whole behind.[47] God's re-creation of the world is not yet complete, but in Christ and his body, the church, *it has begun.* The second line in verse 17 is most important for this understanding: "the old has gone, the new has come!" Paul here uses the vocabulary of the Greek translation of Isaiah 43:18. Isaiah 43:18–21 refers to the renewal of the entire creation, including the natural world:

> Remember not the former things,
>   nor consider *the old things.*
> *Behold* I will do *new things.*
>   which will presently spring forth. . . .
> I will make a way in the desert,
>   and rivers in the dry land.
> The beasts of the field will bless me,
>   the owls and young ostriches;
> for I have given water in the desert,
>   and rivers in the dry land,
> to give drink to my chosen race,
>   my people whom I have preserved
>   to tell forth my praises.[48]

Isaiah 65:17 may also lie behind 2 Corinthians 5:15:

> Behold, I will create
>   new heavens and a new earth.
> The former things will not be remembered,
>   nor will they come to mind.[49]

Love of Neighbor and Care for Creation

What, then, is the significance of this New Testament understanding of creation and resurrection? If the consequences of the resurrection are righteousness and a new creation, what are the implications for life in this present age in which the new creation has been planted in humanity as a seed, waiting that day when all things will be fully transformed? Steck answers quite to the point:

> The world of creation the believer lives in is a world dominated by the madness of man's rejection of God. . . . [But] Christian action is not centered on, or motivated by, fear. Its center is the connection between the divine future and the view of the world as creation. . . . What faith "can" do, by the power of God in Christ, to preserve the world of creation is to perform untiringly token acts as signs, manifestations of the future salvation in the sphere of the natural world, which testify that God has opened his new world for all created things; crystallizations which give concrete form in life to the unity of God, the creator and redeemer, and to the unity of the divine activity directed toward the world.[50]

According to Paul, righteousness is expected of Christians who walk by the Spirit in this present age.[51] This righteousness is summarized as love of one's neighbor, a concept revealed in the Ten Commandments.[52] *But one cannot love one's neighbor without taking care of creation.* Pollution can injure and literally kill one's neighbors. The poor use of natural and other resources represents theft from the neighbor, indeed from our own children and grandchildren, who may someday curse us for this. People destroy the earth and do "wrong to a neighbor" because they covet more than the Creator has allotted to them.[53] This greed, says Paul in Colossians 3:5, is idolatry.[54] Greed is an attitude of worship that dethrones the Creator and elevates the creature to the Creator's place. In Romans 1:25 Paul declares, "They exchanged the truth of God for a lie, and worshiped and served created things rather than the Creator—who is forever praised." The paradoxical point here is that when people reject God and his norms for life, they end up worshiping and defiling the world they idolize.

In contrast to this, Christians are to conduct themselves "decently, as in the daytime, not in orgies and drunkenness, not in sexual immorality and debauchery. . . . Rather, clothe yourselves with the Lord Jesus Christ, and do not think about how to gratify the desires of the sinful nature."[55] In this passage, the keynote for keeping the law is restraint of unbridled human desires.

On the basis of God's free gift of righteousness in Christ, Christians are now empowered by the Spirit and responsible for exhibiting Christ's righteousness in the created world with its goods, its human bodies, and ultimately its lakes, lands, and air.

> For the kingdom of God is not a matter of eating and drinking, but of righteousness, peace and joy in the Holy Spirit. . . . Do not destroy the work of God for the sake of food. All food is clean, but it is wrong for a man to eat anything that causes someone else to stumble. It is better not to eat meat or drink wine or to do anything else that will cause your brother to fall. . . . everything that does not come from faith is sin.[56]

Paul's focus in this text is on Jewish dietary laws,[57] but the implications for the use of the creation in other areas and contexts is plain: "Everything that does not come from faith is sin." As sin infects the entire creation, so also redemption and the obedience of faith extend to every corner of creation: "And *whatever* you do, whether in word or deed, do it all in the name of the Lord Jesus, giving thanks to God the Father through him"[58] [italics added].

The cosmic "new creation" of God begins with those who are "in Christ";[59] so also Paul's ethic begins with a focus on human beings as our neighbors, fellow image-bearers of God. But precisely because our existence is bodily, because we are *ādām* (Hebrew for "man," "mankind," "Adam") from the *ădāmâ* (Hebrew for "earth"), earthlings from the earth, the New Testament Christian ethic cannot, and does not ignore God's good creation. Love for the neighbor cannot exist without love for the earth.

And yet, love for nonhuman creatures would be distorted if it were only an indirect way of loving other humans. God's creatures are good and to be loved according to their natures. The glory and splendor of God's works are quite obviously not restricted to the human species. The moon and the stars, the lily and the raven, the rain and the woods are all beautiful in themselves. Both Jesus and Paul refer to their created glory,[60] a glory that praises God and delights God's image-bearers, man and woman. "For from him and through him and to him are all things. To him be the glory forever! Amen."[61]

4

The Kingdom of God

and Stewardship of Creation

Gordon Zerbe

God reigns; let the earth rejoice.

Psalm 97:1

Thy kingdom come . . . on earth as it is in heaven.

Matthew 6:10

Nowhere does the New Testament directly call for the care of the earth. At the same time, the New Testament is by no means silent on the matter of humanity's relationship to creation. The New Testament projects a vision of the kingdom of God that is full of implications for a Christian environmental ethic.[1]

The theme of the kingdom of God is particularly promising for articulating the ecological meaning of the New Testament since it is as comprehensive a symbol of

73

salvation as can be found in the New Testament. The
kingdom of God is a central theme from the Gospels to
Revelation. Even Paul stresses the theme in key passages,
and the core of Paul's theology points to that final triumph
of God throughout the cosmos already inaugurated in
Christ.[2]

The vision of the kingdom in the New Testament
focuses on human redemption in both personal and social
terms. It incorporates many dimensions of salvation,
including those of resurrection, eternal life, and justification. But this vision also encompasses the restoration of
the earth and the entire universe. The social dimensions of
the kingdom have been critical for articulating social
aspects of Christian ethics.[3] In this essay we will inquire
as to how the cosmic dimensions of the kingdom provide
a grounding for a Christian environmental ethic.

The problems of a kingdom-oriented theology and ethic
of creation, however, must also be acknowledged. First,
the kingdom in the New Testament has a distinctly apocalyptic shape. When some Christians interpret this apocalyptic perspective to mean that salvation is essentially
individual, spiritual, heavenly, and next-worldly, do not
passivity, pessimism, and escapism in regard to social and
earthly life become biblically justified? Why preserve the
present earth when it is headed for collapse and a new
heaven and new earth will replace it? Why be concerned
with the earth at all? Are not spiritual concerns more
important?[4] Second, from the other side of the theological spectrum there are increasing challenges to the monarchical view of the God-world relationship in Scripture and
in Christian theology. Is not this view, it is argued, both
obsolete and dangerous for our time?[5]

After considering the theme of the kingdom of God in
the Old Testament and Jewish apocalyptic thought, the
implications of the New Testament vision of the kingdom for a theology and ethic of creation will be drawn,
and some of the remaining problems associated with such
an approach will be addressed.

The Kingdom of God in the Old Testament

It is necessary to consider the origins of the tradition of the kingdom for three reasons. First, Jesus in the Gospels nowhere defines the kingdom of God, apparently because it was already familiar to his audience from the prophetic hope of the Old Testament and its development in Jewish apocalypticism.[6] Second, it is important to see the continuity between the vision of the kingdom in the Old Testament and the New Testament. Even if there are some changes in this vision, it is a false dichotomy to cut off the New Testament from its Old Testament sources. Third, the kingdom of God in the New Testament is dependent on Jewish apocalyptic thought, even as it transforms this perspective.[7] Jewish apocalyptic thought provides the missing link between the perspectives of the Old Testament and the New Testament, and it is necessary to understand particularly the social and political dynamics behind this shift.

The kingdom of God was a developing and multifaceted concept, and it is impossible to trace all of its variations.[8] Some key points may be observed. Throughout the Bible, the kingdom of God generally refers to the dynamic and kingly rule of God, not especially to a sphere or place in which this rule operates, although this latter aspect occasionally emerges.

According to the Old Testament, God's rule is eternal and universal.[9] This is expressed most basically in the creation of the universe wherein God gained victory over the powers of chaos.[10] God's rule thus extends over the entire earth.[11] Not only is creation an expression of God's rule, but continuing order in the natural and human worlds is also based on God's kingship. Thus, affronts to and rebellion from God's rule cause breakdowns in the natural and cosmic order.[12] While this is apparent especially in the fall,[13] attacks from political enemies are also pictured as a rise in the primeval powers of chaos, the floods.[14] Thus God's rule is what maintains order in creation.

God's rule was thought to be manifested especially in Israel's historical existence; in fact, Israel's existence was also believed to be an act of divine creation. While God was the supreme King on Zion, Israel's regent was understood as God's adopted son and representative with the task of ensuring that God's rule of righteousness and justice was realized.

But the kingdom of God also appears in the Old Testament, particularly in the prophetic tradition, as a hope for the future. Because of a lack of justice and faithfulness to the covenant, the prophets during the time of Israel's monarchies proclaimed that God would come to judge and battle God's own people. Out of this would come a new order of righteousness.[15] Later, in the experience of exile, wherein the plain and painful reality was obvious that the rule of God was not universally recognized, the hope for a new and golden age of worldwide peace, justice, and harmony under God's rule emerged with a new urgency and grandeur.

This vision appears most impressively in the announcement in Isaiah 40–66 of a new exodus and a new creation out of the chaos. These chapters in Isaiah express that perception of a new heaven and earth wherein nature is rejuvenated, long life and peace are enjoyed, warfare and predatory relationships in nature are ended, fellowship with God is restored, the peace and paradise of Eden is regained, and sorrow is banished.[16] The kingdom of God means a redeemed earth; earth is the scene and object of the kingdom of God. This vision of Isaiah was to play an important role in further reflection on the kingdom in Jewish apocalyptic thought and New Testament writings.[17]

The prophetic hope of the Old Testament, then, is for the earthly establishment of the kingdom of God by the breaking in of God into history.[18] Human society and the very structure of the world would be disrupted;[19] but the result would be a new and transformed order, redeemed from all corruption and evil.

The fortunes of Israel in Palestine, however, did not improve. Beginning in the third century B.C., out of the crucible of alienation, persecution, and martyrdom, and under the influence of Persian and Greek ideas, this prophetic hope was sharpened into what is described as apocalyptic thought.[20] Out of the attempt to reconcile faith in a sovereign and benevolent God with the experience of evil and suffering in this world, a new understanding of the kingdom developed. Increasingly, the kingdom was seen as a hope beyond history and this world, which was totally dominated by evil powers. What was lost was a dynamic concept of God's redemptive activity in history.

The shape of Jewish apocalyptic hope, which flourished from 200 B.C. to A.D. 100, can be summarized under three headings.[21] First, we need to consider historical dualism, the concept of the two ages. A radical discontinuity was seen between this age or world and the age to come; salvation was expected beyond history, not within history. A kind of cosmological dualism emerged: The present world is in the grip of two conflicting spirits, God and Satan. The course of historical and cosmic events was seen in terms of angelic forces; in particular, the forces of evil seemed to have the upper hand. But this cosmological dualism was limited by a temporal dualism: The struggle was limited to the present age, at the end of which God would triumph completely and inaugurate the age to come. This historical and cosmological dualism sometimes verged on a metaphysical dualism, in which the cosmos and physical existence themselves were seen as inherently evil. But this step was never made.

Second, some had a universal cosmic expectation, seen as a radical transformation of the world order. The end was seen as a vast cosmic catastrophe; the present order, including creation, would crumble under the weight of sin and evil. But through an act issuing from the throne of God, a new order would be inaugurated and present ("earthly") conditions would be overthrown. The whole cosmos would be restored, returned to the state of creation (though some writings refer to a complete replacement of the old world);[22] the faithful would be resurrected to enjoy eternal life, while the unfaithful and impious would suffer eternal damnation (the idea of the afterlife develops at this time); and the kingdom of God would be manifest visibly on earth. While some writers saw the kingdom in more transcendental, heavenly terms,[23] most saw it as an earthly existence freed from all corruption. Indeed, the arrival of the kingdom meant the amalgamation of the heavenly and earthly spheres—the original "glory" of creation would be realized on earth.[24]

Third, some expected the imminent end and transformation of the world. Evidence of cosmic decay, in both the natural and social orders, was seen as a sign of the imminence of the final onslaught of evil and the arrival of the new order.

To summarize, in Jewish apocalyptic thought, as based on the prophetic hope of the Old Testament, the end was seen as one imminent, cataclysmic, world-ending and re-creating manifestation of the kingly rule of God; the new order coming was the kingdom of God. This worldview provides the framework for the theology of the kingdom in the New Testament. It is inaccurate to say that the Jewish hope for the kingdom was merely political and that Jesus proclaimed a new spiritual or heavenly kingdom.

Four categories may characterize the meaning of the kingdom in the New Testament: (1) the kingdom of God as a vision of future salvation; (2) the kingdom as a present reality of salvation; (3) the kingdom as a new order of conduct; and (4) the kingdom as evident in a new, redeemed community.[25]

Before these four dimensions of the kingdom can be grasped, however, it is necessary to observe a fundamental presupposition of the New Testament: God's rule is exemplified in the creation of the universe. Creation is not a common theme in the New Testament, but it is implied everywhere. The connection between God's eternal rule and creation is pictured most impressively in John the seer's throne vision. At the climax of the scene, twenty-four ministering elders "lay their crowns before the throne" and sing: "You are worthy, our Lord and God, to receive glory and honor and power, for you created all things, and by your will they were created and have their being."[26] In this and other passages,[27] the New Testament affirms with the Old Testament the createdness and goodness of the entire universe. As in the Old Testament, the lordship of God (and of Christ) is expressed most fundamentally in creation.[28] When the other aspects of the kingdom in the New Testament are examined, this perspective must always be remembered.

The Kingdom as a Vision of Future Salvation

One of the primary meanings of the kingdom of God in the New Testament is that of a new order in the age to come in which the redeemed participate.[29] Nowhere in the New Testament is the precise shape or character of this future order extensively defined; yet, the basic contours of this vision can be discerned. Most fundamentally—and in continuity with the prophetic-apocalyptic hope—the kingdom of God entails the restoration of the entire cosmos to its original state; that is, it is a renewal of creation. When God's rule is finally realized throughout the universe, a new order of righteousness, peace, harmony, and nature's renewal will emerge. In 1 Corinthians 15:24–28 Paul writes that in the end Christ's and God's rule will be achieved throughout the universe "so that God may be all in all." In the end, there will be no more separation between the earthly and heavenly realms.[30]

The transformation that results from God's final triumph is comprehensive—personal, social, and cosmic. It entails the restoration of all disorder and broken relationships resulting from the invasion of sin (Satan) into the world.[31]

On the personal level, it means resurrection—the redemption of bodily life[32]—through the final defeat of the power of death.[33] Life, bodily life, was the original intent of creation.[34]

On the social level, the kingdom also means restoration. In Romans 14:17 Paul describes the kingdom of God with three Greek terms: *dikaiosynē* ("righteousness"), *eirēnē* ("peace"), and *chara* ("joy"). These are loaded terms. The former two are key terms expressing the idea of the kingdom of God in the Old Testament.[35] *Dikaiosynē* in its most basic sense means things or people being in right relationship: this can mean personal righteousness, but also social justice. The Bible does not distinguish finely between them. *Eirēnē* here signifies the Hebrew concept of *šālôm*: peace, harmony, wholeness, prosperity, physical well-being.[36] Joy is the natural expression of feeling when justice (or righteousness) and peace are experienced. To express this new social reality in the coming kingdom, the New Testament frequently uses the image of the banquet, a harmonious table fellowship where all are satisfied.[37] It goes without saying that an integral part of this social restoration is unimpeded and direct fellowship with Christ and God.[38]

The vision of the coming kingdom does not stop here but reaches out to embrace the entire cosmos. The entirety of creation is affected and returned to its original state. In continuity with the vision of Isaiah 65–66, the New Testament affirms that the final realization of God's rule means a new heaven and a new earth. According to John the seer, once God's rule is fully established[39] and all God's enemies who are responsible for the destruction of the earth have been destroyed,[40] a new heaven and a new earth will emerge.[41] Just as the throne vision of Revelation 4 culminated in a reference to creation, an act of re-creation now emerges from the throne: "He who was seated on the throne said, 'I am making everything [i.e., the entire universe] new!'"[42]

Accordingly, Revelation 22:1–5 pictures the kingdom of God in which God's people "shall reign for ever and ever" as an Edenic paradise, a return to primeval time before the invasion of sin. As it is phrased in 2 Peter 3:13, "But in keeping with his promise we are looking forward to a new heaven and a new earth, the home of righteousness."

Peter's speech in Acts 3 also contains an important reference to this cosmic restoration. Verse 21 refers to the ultimate *chronoi apokatastaseōs pantōn*, "the time . . . to restore everything." What is remarkable about this phrase is that it is also used by the historian Diodorus (1st cent. B.C.) to refer to the restoration of the whole cosmos to perfection, including the reversion of the stars to their original orbit or starting place.[43] It is also noteworthy that this passage implies that this restoration is an earthly reality, mediated through the return of the Messiah.

Perhaps the most important reference to this cosmic restoration is in Romans 8:18–25. Here Paul describes the coming "glory," which is a synonym for the coming kingdom of God.[44] All creation is restored: People are redeemed to whole, bodily life, and nonhuman creation is set free from the bondage it is suffering under the weight of evil. Indeed, these two aspects of redemption—human and cosmic—are integrally related; one does not happen without the other.[45]

Other passages in Paul's letters confirm the importance for him of this comprehensive renewal of creation in Christ. Paul speaks of "the new creation,"[46] the reconciliation of the cosmos,[47] and the new humanity "being renewed in knowledge after the image of its Creator."[48] While these texts refer to human redemption in particular, it is clear that for Paul these notions embraced all of nonhuman creation as well.[49] When he speaks of the reconciliation or justification of "everything" in Christ,[50] Paul refers to the final cosmic transformation. Not surprisingly, then, Paul claims that the Abrahamic promise to his descendants in faith involves the inheritance of the cosmos.[51]

Three final passages confirm that restored humanity's proper habitat is earth; future salvation is not a disembodied spiritual existence in a transcendent heaven. (1) "Blessed are the meek, for they will inherit the earth."[52] It is important to realize that "inheriting the earth" in Matthew's beatitudes is equated with receiving the kingdom.[53] Here, significantly, it is the meek who will inherit the earth in God's future reign. Those who will care for the earth in a nondomineering, nondegrading way are the ones who are truly qualified to inherit the earth. (2) "You have made them to be a kingdom and priests to serve our God, and they will reign on the earth."[54] In this hymn to the slain but victorious Lamb, the final vindication of God's people in the kingdom is seen as a new order on earth. This is not simply a reference to a temporary state in a millennial kingdom before the consummation,[55] but to the final kingdom, when God's people are co-regents with God in the service of God's re-creation.[56] (3) "Your kingdom come, your will be done on earth as it is in heaven."[57] This prayer is critically important for a kingdom theology of earthkeeping. It has a double reference: It refers to the hope for the future transformation of all things in a new creation, and to the hope for the arrival of God's order in the present world. In both cases, the prayer affirms that humanity's proper habitat in the kingdom, as in creation, is earth. This idea is foundational for a New Testament theology and ethic of creation. Unfortunately, much misunderstanding has arisen from Matthew's preference for the phrase "kingdom of heaven," which seems to identify the kingdom simply as a heavenly reality. But the "kingdom of heaven" is synonymous with "kingdom of God." Here "heaven" is a circumlocution to avoid using the name of God and implies nothing about the character of the kingdom.

To summarize, in continuity with the concept of the kingdom in the Old Testament prophets and in Jewish apocalyptic thought, the New Testament vision of the kingdom is first that of the new order in the age to come. That reality results when the rule of Christ and of God is realized in all creation. In radical discontinuity with the present order (which is marred by sin and largely controlled by demonic powers), the kingdom is a vision of things as they ought to be in the entire cosmos, both human and nonhuman. As the most comprehensive symbol of salvation in the New Testament, it entails the restoration of all disorder in creation. It is an order in which all things are in right relationship, an order in which righteousness dwells. While the focus of the kingdom of God in the New Testament is on human redemption, the final restoration of humanity is inseparably linked with the ultimate restoration of all creation. The definitive vision of salvation is that of a redeemed community of whole persons set within the context of a restored creation. It is personal, social, and cosmic in scope. This future vision shows that God is concerned not only with the world of humanity, but with the entirety of creation. All creation is good and is the object of God's ultimate redeeming act.

The Kingdom as a Present Reality of Redemption

The kingdom of God, however, is not simply a future order of salvation. The Christian confession is that in Christ, God's rule has already broken into the present order so that one can speak of the presence of the future.[58] Even though the kingdom will be consummated in the future, it has already been inaugurated in this age. In Christ, the end has become decisive and definitive for the present. Herein lies the Christian transformation of Jewish apocalyptic thought.

The importance of the presence of the kingdom for a theology and ethic of creation can hardly be overestimated. Without this affirmation Christian faith could easily degenerate into a posture of spiritually preoccupied escapism and total pessimism regarding the present world. Christian faith must affirm the ongoing redemption within and through the present spiritual-physical, social, and cosmic order. The New Testament speaks of the present experience of redemption exclusively in terms of the human realm; but insofar as this redemption is defined by ultimate redemption, it follows that the nonhuman world must also be included in the vision of present transformation, a transformation that is inaugurated by Christ and advanced by his followers.

According to the synoptic Gospels, the kingdom of God is dynamically present in the life and mission of Jesus. It is particularly in healing—-through the victory over the evil powers which corrupt this age—that the kingdom is manifest.[59] The kingdom is something that people must presently receive[60] and is said to be within or among people.[61] The kingdom and its righteousness ought to be sought[62] and to be prayed for as a present, earthly reality.[63] Not only is it manifest when individuals acknowledge God's rule by faithful obedience, it is also a new social order of righteousness and justice. The kingdom is not simply an individual, spiritual, internal, invisible rule or reality.

In the teaching of Jesus, then, the kingdom of God is the central symbol for the new vision of life in its fulness. It is an order in sharp contrast to the present order. As Donald Kraybill puts it, it is an "upside-down kingdom."[64] It means radical inclusiveness, particularly of the outcasts and powerless,[65] destabilization of the world's order of domination and inequality,[66] and nonhierarchical relationships through the ministry of servanthood.[67] Finally, insofar as Jesus' life and conduct is a parable of the kingdom, we can see self-giving care for people and for creation inherent in God's new order.[68]

The apostle Paul also affirms that in Christ the coming age has already invaded the present world. In particular, the resurrection of Jesus is the turning point, announcing and validating the imminent arrival of the kingdom and already effecting changes in the present.[69] Thus Paul can talk about the fact that God has already "rescued us from the dominion of darkness and brought us into the kingdom of the son he loves" immediately after a statement about the future inheritance of Christians.[70] Also, when Paul speaks of the kingdom as righteousness, peace, and joy,[71] the addition of the words "in the Holy Spirit" confirms that he is speaking of the presence of the future kingdom. Through Christ, the powers of this age have already been vanquished for the Christian.[72] Because the future renewal of all things has already begun to transform the present, Paul can refer to being "in Christ" as already effecting a "new creation," the "reconciliation of the world," and the renewal of the original image of God.[73] Finally, Paul sees Christians as "fellow workers for the kingdom of God."[74] While the kingdom is fundamentally God's act of redemption, Christians are coworkers in it. Thus, Paul says that while the reconciliation of the cosmos is God's ministry in Christ, this same ministry has been given to Paul and his co-workers.[75]

To summarize, the presence of the kingdom means that the restoration of creation's wholeness has already begun in a real, evident, and substantial way, yet the kingdom will not be manifested in its totality and perfection until the future.

The implications of this reality for the care of creation must be observed. Admittedly, the New Testament articulates the present reality of the kingdom or salvation only in terms of human redemption, whether personal or corporate. Nevertheless, the ideal of the presence of the kingdom has clear implications for the present concern for the earth's healing. As Francis Schaeffer explained in 1970, when we carry these ideas [of substantial healing in the present] over into the area of our relationship with nature, there is an exact parallel. On the basis of the fact that there is going to be total redemption in the future, not only of [humanity] but of all creation, the Christian who believes the Bible should be the [person] who—with God's help and in the power of the Holy Spirit—is treating nature now in the direction of the way nature will be then. . . . God's calling to the Christian now, and to the Christian community, in the area of nature—just as it is in the area of personal Christian living in true spirituality—is that we should exhibit a substantial healing here and now, between [humanity] and nature and nature and itself, as far as Christians can bring it to pass.[76]

There are perhaps two main reasons why the New Testament does not specifically address this calling, even though its view of redemption seems to imply it. First, at the time of the development of the Christian Scriptures, the degradation of creation through human action had not yet occurred to a significant extent. Second, at that time nature appeared to be more powerful than humans, controllable only by God, and thus was not in view as the object of present redemption. In the face of environmental and nuclear crises, neither of these conditions hold today. The present situation makes it imperative for Christians to see natural creation itself as the object of needed redemptive action inaugurated through Christ and pursued by Christ's followers.

In particular, the vision of restoration in the coming kingdom defines the present tasks of redemptive action. The futurity of the kingdom is not an occasion for escapism, passivity, or pessimism; rather, the coming kingdom guides and motivates present responsibilities in and for creation. Since the kingdom is both present and future, the believer lives in the balance between the already and the not yet of salvation. Living within this tension keeps the believer from both passive pessimism and excessive optimism regarding the realization of redemption in this age.[77] Even if ultimate redemption is unattainable before the end, the Christian continues to work redemptively to make the kingdom a reality in this age.

The Kingdom as a New Order of Conduct

Just as presence and futurity are integrally linked in the New Testament idea of the kingdom, so are a new ethics and new community. The latter two follow from the former two: ethics and community are based on God's act of redemption in Christ. The first two aspects of the kingdom have primarily a gift character, and so the call is to receive the kingdom. But the kingdom also entails a demand: the right relationships that will characterize the coming kingdom must be pursued in the present world. Matthew 6:33 expresses this third aspect: "But seek first [God's] kingdom and his righteousness." Indeed, the manifestation of true righteousness is a condition for entrance into the coming kingdom.[78]

The new order of kingdom ethics is summarized most comprehensively by the term "righteousness." Righteousness is defined by the nature of the kingdom; it means relationships, attitudes, and conduct appropriate to the kingdom's present and future manifestation through God's act. John 18:36 provides an important example of kingdom ethics: "Jesus said, 'My kingdom is not of this world. If it were, my servants would fight. . . . But now my kingdom is from another place.'"

First, kingdom ethics are in radical discontinuity with the ethics of this world. The dualism evident here is an ethical dualism—Christ's kingdom does not have the character of being from this world. It is not that the kingdom is purely spiritual and without worldly relevance. Second, in kingdom ethics, means and ends are in harmony.[79] The ways of the future kingdom are already in effect. Thus, kingdom citizens use the means of peacemaking and nonviolence as appropriate to the new era of peace; and they

live life-styles that exhibit care of creation as appropriate
to the new era of cosmic re-creation.

The righteousness of the kingdom (right relationships in
the new and coming age) is comprehensive. Typically,
Christians have narrowed the meaning of the term "righteousness" to refer simply to personal morality—private
and interpersonal righteousness. But the righteousness of
the kingdom also explicitly involves a new social ethic of
justice: right relationships among groups. Thus, the kingdom citizen promotes peacemaking[80] and rejects the use of
violence.[81]

Kingdom ethics go even further to imply an environmental ethic. Insofar as sin has caused a brokenness in
humanity's relationships with nature, and insofar as the
restoration of all nonhuman creation is included in the
coming kingdom, it necessarily follows that righteousness includes a restored relationship with creation. Kingdom righteousness necessarily implies ecojustice. The
ethic of peacemaking, *shalom*-building, and nonviolence
must be extended to embrace the relationship with creation.[82] Though this notion is not explicit in the New Testament, biblical texts imply it. Isaiah's vision of restored
humanity and nature climaxes with the statement that
there will no longer be any hurt or destruction.[83] And
John's vision of judgment states that those who destroy
the earth will ultimately be destroyed.[84] Revelation 19:2
shows preeminently that God is concerned about creation
and human actions toward it.[85]

But we should not think that this last aspect of ecological righteousness is unrelated to other aspects of righteousness. As many writers have observed,[86] in the contemporary world the ecological crisis is intimately tied
to the problem of social justice. Just as social domination
is interconnected with the domination of nature, an ethic
of care for creation must be integrally related to an ethic
of social justice. A kingdom ethic based on the restoration
of all creation helps cohere personal, social, and ecological
ethics.

The Kingdom as a New Community under Christ's Lordship

The notion of the presence of God's kingly rule necessarily implies a realm or community in which this rule is exercised. While the kingdom of God is not equated with the church in the New Testament, the idea of a community that has submitted to the rule of God manifest in Jesus implies the notion of the church. The church, then, is that new community which seeks to order its life in terms of the gift and demands of the kingdom. It seeks to model the new order of God's rule in its present existence. The new community accordingly ought to be that social reality that demonstrates a new relationship to creation.

According to the New Testament, the community of the king stands in sharp contrast to the present order. Two images characterize the church's outward mission: Kingdom citizens are a light in the world,[87] and fertilizer for the earth.[88] First, those people who are under God's rule have a witnessing character in the world that encourages people to praise God. When this idea is applied to the problem of Christianity and ecology, it means that the church's care for creation will encourage people to praise the Creator. Second, as "fertilizer" the new community has a rejuvenating or life-giving effect to the earth. The church has the task of pursuing redemptive activity in the present order. While "earth" in this text refers to the world of humanity, a more literal reading of the terms may also be appropriate. The church must see part of its redemptive mission as helping to restore the degradation of creation.

Remaining Problems

Two questions critical to the theme of creation stewardship remain: (1) the problem of the presumed temporality of the present earth, and (2) the tendency in Christian theology to transmute the temporal horizon of redemption into a spatial one.

Is not the present world passing away to make way for a new heaven and earth? If so, why do people need to be concerned about the present state of the earth?

It is true that many New Testament texts refer to the "passing away" of heaven and earth, based on Isaiah 51:6.[89] But the following points should be noted. First, as in Jewish apocalyptic, one can also discern two trends in the New Testament in the interpretation of the cosmic restoration of Isaiah 65:17. Some texts imply a destruction and replacement of the old world;[90] but the Pauline references imply a restoration of the present world.[91] Thus Paul says that "this world in its present form (schēma) is passing away."[92] The New Testament itself is in dialogue on this question.

Second, the problem is not with the creation itself, but with sin. Earth is being crushed under the weight of human sin and evil powers. Thus the images of the earth's passing are those more of refinement and purification—to rid creation of evil—than of outright destruction and replacement.[93] Moreover, God's interest in creation is evident in the promise that those who destroy the earth will themselves be destroyed.[94]

Third, even the ideas of refinement or replacement do not necessarily mean that one should not care for the present creation. One can point to the resurrection as a parallel. The body is destroyed and raised with a new resurrection body; but this does not mean that one is no longer to care for the present physical body. Moreover, whether the old cosmos is restored or replaced, redeemed humanity is always on a redeemed earth—earth is humanity's proper habitat.[95]

Fourth, the present reality of redemption implies that the cosmos is the object of God's reconciling work, just as the present body is the place of ongoing redemption. There is no biblical basis for disregarding and degrading the state of the earth because of it future restoration.[96]

A second problem is the tendency of Christian theology to soften the future-oriented focus of cosmic salvation through an emphasis on spiritual or heavenly salvation. It is the loss of the tension between the present age and the age to come that results in a diminishment of salvation as a cosmic and earthly reality. When the temporal tension of this age and the age to come is diminished, the primary contrast becomes spatial—earthly versus heavenly or spiritual.[97] According to the New Testament, heaven is indeed where God's rule is now recognized. The constant affirmation, however, is that this rule will ultimately be manifested throughout the entire cosmos so that redeemed life will be fully experienced on a redeemed earth. The final hope of Christians is not heaven, but participation in God's restoration of all things. This is the ultimate vision that informs the present task of Christians in the world.

The kingdom of God, the central theme running through the New Testament, has significant implications for the care of creation. As a comprehensive vision for future salvation, the kingdom entails the renewal of all creation, human and natural. This expectation is holistic: it affirms the spiritual-physical unity of the person; it relates personal and social renewal; it inseparably links human and cosmic aspects of redemption; it affirms the interconnectedness of the spiritual and material dimensions of life; and it means the ultimate unity of all things, including heaven and earth, so that God is all in all. The kingdom unites creation and redemption—redemption as re-creation focuses back on the original creation. In continuity with the Old Testament and Jewish apocalyptic hopes for the kingdom, this New Testament hope sees the proper habitat for redeemed humanity on a redeemed earth. Thus the kingdom in the New Testament is not a merely spiritual or heavenly reality.

But the New Testament also affirms that in Christ the kingdom has invaded the present. Moreover, the kingdom is not only a new order of salvation, but a new order of relationships and conduct. The presence of the kingdom means that Christians should order their lives in terms of the values and shape of the new and coming kingdom. Since the righteousness of the kingdom means right relationships appropriate to the new and coming order, Christians are led directly to an ethic of care for the creation. Moreover, while the kingdom is fundamentally God's act of salvation, the New Testament calls Christians to be co-workers in the building of the kingdom, which includes the redemption and healing of humanity and creation.

A proper understanding of the kingly rule of God does not allow Christians to escape the present but calls them to be co-workers for the realization of God's rule in and for creation. Instead of providing an occasion for the disregard and degradation of creation, the future vision of the kingdom defines and motivates present ministries of reconciliation, including earthkeeping. When God reigns in the hearts of people and ultimately throughout the cosmos, the earth will indeed rejoice.

5

Creation's Care and Keeping

in the Life of Jesus

Vernon Visick

When I was a child growing up in an evangelical Christian community in California, we tended to pay more attention to the "work" of Jesus than to his "life." By "work" we meant the death and especially the resurrection of Jesus, which to us was the center of the faith. "The Son of Man must be delivered into the hands of sinful men, be crucified and on the third day be raised again."[1]

To be sure, we had been told that in his everyday life Jesus was in every way like we were, but without sin, and that his life was a model for ours. But for a perfect, sinless life to end in death on the cross seemed to us more a matter of "bad news" than "good news." So we tended to focus on what we felt the more central truth, the death and resurrection of Christ.

Our focus on the "work" of Christ was reinforced by what we felt to be the weakness and wrongheadedness of liberals who *did* pay attention to the life of Jesus. The way in which they focused on the life of Jesus seemed to be a substitute for belief in the reality of the death and resurrection of Jesus. Yet conservative Christians, realizing that the life of Jesus was more attractive to non-Christians than assertions about doctrine, also focused on the life of Jesus, usually for apologetic reasons and not without some distortions. Inevitably, however, these efforts at interpreting the life of Jesus did not seem to be able to avoid ideological elements, and thus we were subjected to Jesus the perfect salesman, Jesus the supporter of capitalist society, Jesus the positive thinker and achiever par excellence, Jesus the liberal reformer, and later, Jesus the radical revolutionary. The end result strengthened the resolution of conservatives to preach the pure gospel and avoid the temptations involved in clarifying the relationship between the life of Jesus and his time—and of ours.

The result of these complex dynamics was ambiguous: We offered a spirituality that was relevant to ultimate matters of life and death, but only partially relevant or even irrelevant to the everyday work of caring for and keeping the world in which God had placed us. We were so heavenly minded that we were of little earthly good.[2]

The judgment that those who take seriously the transcendent meaning of the Christian faith are somehow less competent in the management and preservation of earthly affairs is not of recent vintage. It was the charge hurled against the Christians during the latter days of the Roman Empire, and it is a charge periodically revived by those who feel that Christians are never fully committed to their particular cause.

In contrast, each of the essays in this volume argue that the New Testament *is* relevant for the solution of the environmental crisis, that a true grasp of faith leads us to a vision of harmony between human beings and nature, and that the new life that has come to us through our relationship to Jesus Christ implies power to achieve that vision. The question remains, however, does the New Testament shed any light on the practical question of how we get from our present state to what ought to be? Does the New Testament—and in particular, the life of Jesus—suggest to us an effective, politically relevant method for responding to the ecological crisis? Or must we abide with those who set themselves right with God through Jesus Christ, but get their political ethics from either the Old Testament or contemporary political thinking?

If we approach Jesus' life with a historical consciousness, with a willingness to reconsider the categories and questions that we unconsciously bring to our understanding of him, and if we are willing to follow him in the systematic, disciplined, and creative way in which Jesus approached his own tradition and the problems he faced, then we will have something profound and practical to offer in the struggle to deal responsibly with the environmental crisis, something that may be crucial to its resolution.[3]

God has manifested his grace to us not only in the death and resurrection of Christ, but also in the actual, everyday details of the life of Jesus.

At first glance, the assertion that Jesus provides us with an absolutely crucial method for approaching the environmental crisis would seem to be a reckless assertion. A quick survey of the Gospels reveals that Jesus did not say much about the environment. Since most of the problems Jesus addresses seem to be people-related problems, it is not clear how the Gospels might be relevant to the ecological crisis. While the solution to the environmental crisis would seem to demand political solutions, Jesus is not political in the contemporary sense of the term. This may explain the tendency of Christian ecologists to base their ecological work on the Old Testament.

Although Jesus' ecological ethic is not prominent in the text of the Gospels, the fact is that Jesus, as a Jew, lived a profound ecological ethic. He demonstrated a practical way of dealing with problems that is relevant to the solution of *any* practical problem, including those of contemporary ecological politics. Also, he was aware of the political dynamics of his time and showed himself astute in relating to those political circumstances. As we shall see, the life of Jesus is quite relevant to the solution of our environmental problems.

The Jewish Approach to the Environment: *Stewardship*

Jesus mentions nature in only a few places: (1) in a contrast between the beauty of flowers and Solomon in all of his grandeur, concluding that flowers are more beautiful;[4] and (2) in a comparison between the respective value of sparrows and human beings, asserting that in God's mind human beings are more important than sparrows.[5] Of course, two verses do not provide a comprehensive ecological ethic, yet they do help to clarify Jesus' relationship to nature. Jesus is no technological optimist, overlooking and undervaluing nature in contrast to the wonder of human creativity; nor is he an adherent to Jainism, diminishing the value and centrality of human life by putting all created beings on the same level.

Given the paucity of texts that describe Jesus' attitude toward nature, we must investigate the context in which Jesus was operating. Basic to his attitude toward nature is that he was a Jew, an enthusiastic participant in the Jewish social, political, and religious life of his time as well as a critic of it. As David Ehrenfeld and others have recently demonstrated, the Jews had a profound ecological ethic. Thus, Jesus was immersed in an ethos that nurtured a certain earthiness and positive enjoyment of life, including the appreciation of work, food, and sexuality.[6] This ethos also supported a matrix of ideas that if "man does evil, nature reacts,"[7] that "there is a definite order to the world ordained by God as part of creation. . . . [and that] Nothing was created for no purpose or in vain,"[8] and that "one does not get something for nothing" in the interaction between humans and the world, including the natural world. Jewish society during Jesus' time was permeated with a general awareness of human dependence upon and interdependence with nature.

An ethos, however, does not itself make an ethic; ethics is a matter of rational reflection on the structure and meaning implied in the ethos. When Jewish religious leaders attempted to articulate the ethical meaning of the ethos in which they existed, they developed the idea of stewardship, namely, that we must be responsible for the human beings, animals, and nature in the midst of which God has placed us. Jesus shared in the common Jewish belief of responsibility toward the created order. He too embraced the idea of stewardship, that creation is not ours to exploit as we wish, but rather belongs to God. As a Jew, he knew that he was not free to abuse the creation or tend only to his private affairs, but that his job was to dress and keep the world for God.

A principle, however, is abstract and needs to be worked out concretely in the everyday life of the community. The means by which the Jewish community tried to live out the ideal of stewardship was the practice of the law, and it is clear from the Gospel record that Jesus was an enthusiastic participant in it. For the Jewish community, the law applied not only to a person's relationship to God and others, but also to the natural world. Thus the law included specific instructions to guide human behavior toward natural resources, animals, and other aspects of nature. Ehrenfeld calls the law a kind of "Steward's Manual" for the care of creation.[9]

The general principle of stewardship was worked out in terms of three subsidiary principles: (1) *bal tashit* (do not destroy); (2) the prohibition against inflicting *za'ar baalei hayyim* (pain of living things); and (3) most of all, the keeping of the Sabbath, including the keeping of the Sabbath year and possibly even the Jubilee.[10]

On the basis of both historical research and reasonable conjecture, therefore, we may assume that Jesus personally lived a profoundly ecological ethic, even though it was kept in the background in the context of Jesus' particular historical situation. If we did nothing else but retrieve the ecological ethic by which Jesus lived and adapt it to our own situation, we could make a significant contribution to the solution of the environmental crisis.

Jesus and the Problem of the Law

If the environmental ethic implied by his Jewish context were all that Jesus had to offer us in our contemporary ecological crisis, those Christians who find their ecological ethics in the Old Testament might seem to be vindicated. There the Jewish ecological ethic is much more explicit. But Jesus has something important to offer just at the point where received tradition is applied to a particular, concrete, and historically different situation. If we are to avoid the problems of legalism and romanticism, we must pay attention to the life of Jesus in relation to the law.

Why was the law such a prominent feature of Jewish life? Human freedom makes the law necessary. It is the capacity to partially transcend the natural order through speech and technology, the capacity through which humans are enabled to grasp and shape the world into which they have been born. From the biblical point of view, the capacity to choose constitutes not only an opportunity but a problem. The Jews felt that it was not enough simply to choose, but to choose rightly, thinking and acting in such a way as to honor God and to preserve and enhance the life God had given. The guide to choosing rightly was the law. Initially, the law was "written on our hearts," but subsequently stated for us by the great lawgivers, codifiers, and commentators on the law in Israel's history.

The law, therefore, was *a way of life*, a series of rational, patterned actions that, if followed, would preserve, facilitate, and enhance life. The law was intended to preserve the relationship between human beings and God, insider and outsider, male and female, parents and children, rich and poor, people and the land. The law promotes right relationships, right actions, and right patterns in every important area of life. Live according to the law, says the Book of Deuteronomy, and you will have life; violate the law, and you will have destruction and death.

It is the understanding of the law as the essential means toward life which is responsible for the many verses of celebration of the law throughout the Old Testament. The feeling of awe, respect and gratitude is nicely captured in the Psalms: "Your statutes stand firm; holiness adorns your house for endless days, O LORD."[11] The law is seen as a precious gift, a delight, a guide for life.

Like any good thing, however, the law could be corrupted. The spirit of the law could be defeated by adherence to the letter of the law. Rules, once historically appropriate, could in different circumstances overwhelm people with legal observances and divert them from contemporary responsibilities. The law, in its greatness and holiness, might itself be lifted up, and in the process take the place of God. In each of these cases, the law could become ambiguous: historically inappropriate, sometimes applied in opposition to its larger purpose, interfering in the relationship between God and human beings. Thus it was possible that the law could become an impediment to the very thing it was intended to facilitate, the honor of God and the nurturing of life.

We must seek to understand Jesus and his ministry from within the context of these tensions over the law. He performed good by constantly reapplying the law in concrete, practical situations. If we would apply the law even as Jesus did, we would be making progress toward an attempt to address the ecological situation. But how did he do this? First, by penetrating to the essence of the law, he developed a criterion by which to judge one's actions. And that essence, Jesus determined, was simply this: loving God and loving one's neighbor. With this criterion, Jesus could review the received tradition and make a judgment about how, in any particular situation, it achieved its goal. We see Jesus doing this throughout his ministry.

The development and application of a criterion, however, was not sufficient to accomplish Jesus' task. For the law had to be applied in concrete circumstances, circumstances that varied from case to case, that were often quite different than they had been under the patriarchs and the prophets. So Jesus participated in the lives of those with whom he interacted, talked with them, asked them questions. Apart from his general thoughtfulness, the characteristic that stands out is his attentiveness to those with whom he worked, the unfailing dignity with which he treated people, and the life-giving appropriateness of his response to them.

Throughout his relationships, Jesus applied the law in a new way, incorporating the best of the old in terms of the needs of the present, a new way with more truth, justice, and thus more life. Jesus said, "I have not come to destroy [the Law or the Prophets] but to fulfill them" (Matt. 5:17). In so doing he could say, "I am the way and the truth and the life" (John 14:6). In other words, he lived and gave what the law demanded but which others, in their confusion, legalism, and bondage could not achieve on their own.

By dealing with the demands of the law in this fashion, Jesus was moral without being moralistic; he compromised without being compromised; he supported liberty without being a rebel or a conformist; he applied the law without being a legalist; and he was neither a libertine nor a formalist. The law of sin and death was overcome by the law of life, embodied in the person of Jesus Christ.

A Christian ecological ethic must approach problems the way that Jesus did: by critiquing the received way of doing things, by applying solutions in the context of new situations, and by bringing the treasured insights of the past into a creative and life-giving relationship with the present. This approach will keep us from abstract idealism, utopianism, or legalism.

Jesus and the Problem of Politics

Practical action in human affairs always leads to politics, but Jesus' everyday work with people does not seem to be political, at least in a way we can recognize easily. For this reason, many Christians who take the political dimension of life seriously go to the Old Testament for guidance and inspiration, the assumption being that the Prophets offer more help than Jesus. To do this, however, is to miss the relevance of the life of Jesus for politics.

In Jesus' day the average citizen did not have the same opportunity for political participation that Israel and Judah had in earlier days. Israel, Judah, and all other smaller political units had been absorbed into the imperial Roman state, so the center of political power had shifted from Judah to Rome. In his everyday life, Jesus busied himself dealing with practical human problems, and his interactions with the Roman rulers were apparently sporadic. But it is incorrect to draw the conclusion from these circumstances that Jesus separated himself from politics, and that his followers restricted themselves to a strictly interpersonal ministry.

In Jesus' time it was impossible *not* to be political, for the political permeated every aspect of society. Nor was it possible for the religious realm to be separated from the political. Every religious alternative implied a political position, and vice versa. All of the religious options of Jesus' time had both religious and political implications. The Pharisees, the Sadducees, the Zealots, and the

Romans each held to a particular religious-political viewpoint. It could not have been otherwise, for organized community life is inevitably political and has religious roots. Jesus could not have withdrawn from politics even if he had wanted to as long as he was to live among other human beings.[12]

Furthermore, by the way in which Jesus worked with those with whom he came into contact, it was inevitable that Jesus would build a movement, gain power, and in the process become a political issue for the authorities. Jesus dealt with others in astonishing ways, immediately overcoming the universal cynicism and wariness of those inside and outside of political power. The new life that Jesus brought to people increased their power, and this inevitably increased Jesus' own following and power. Jesus' travels around the countryside and his journey to Jerusalem was therefore not just a religious phenomenon but a political one as well, the importance of which was not lost on the religious and political authorities. They reacted to Jesus not just as a religious but as a political threat.[13]

Far from being nonpolitical, as Yoder puts it, Jesus said very little that was not political. But what was the nature of Jesus' politics? It was not a politics of who gets what, when, why and how, a politics of class conflict, or a politics of reconstruction, to name several recent definitions. It was a politics of servanthood. It had two foci: service toward God, expressed primarily in the prophetic attack on the inevitable idolatries of politics, and service toward God's creation, especially those parts diminished, disrupted, or threatened by human activity (the poor, the sick, and the oppressed). Jesus' politics were clearly different from those of the Romans, the Sadducees, the Pharisees, and the Zealots.

Interestingly, Jesus' politics of servanthood gained power quickly, as if the dominant political alternatives had left essential problems unattended. His political success created a new situation: The authorities had to decide whether Jesus could be subsumed within the current system, either through co-optation or containment, or whether he had to be eliminated. Their decision to eliminate him by means of violence was a mark of their weakness rather than their power. And their decision not to receive Jesus and his life-giving and preserving politics was the beginning of their downfall.

In sum, Jesus did not do what he did in private, but out in the open in the only place where it could do any good, in relation to the political life that constituted the community of which he was a part. Living in a pre-modern situation, he was necessarily political. His particular politics were neither those of the Jews under the reign of the Jewish kings, nor our own in liberal democracy. Furthermore, the life-giving, creative manner in which he applied the law was effective in building political power, so that by the end of his three years of ministry he had become a major political threat to the existing powers. And he did it with a politics of servanthood.

Jesus as Our Guide in the Environmental Crisis

What difference might a study of the life of Jesus make if we were to follow him in our attempts to deal with the ecological crisis? Jesus' society was largely agrarian, supplemented by a commercial and money economy. In contrast to our own society, the general level of scientific, technical, and commercial development was quite primitive. Furthermore, the society of Jesus' time was subject to perversion, especially by the aristocratic and military elite. Yet, with corrections, the way of life which Jesus and his compatriots lived could be sustained ecologically and could be practiced by all nations indefinitely.

We, on the other hand, live in a highly organized, complex society built around a highly developed science, technology, and a worldwide mechanism of production and exchange. We have more technical control over nature—and more wealth as a result—than any society in history. The perversions to which our society is susceptible, however, result from the entire society and its desire for the further control of natural processes. It is becoming increasingly clear, however, that our way of life has become destructive of the natural environment. Our society cannot be sustained indefinitely, and it cannot be practiced by all nations without destruction.

We need, therefore, a creative application of the "law" by which we live. We must have a renewed understanding of the principles by which our way of life can be sustained indefinitely. We must critique the idolatries that have blinded us to what we are doing, and we must renew our appreciation for the ethic of stewardship.

In Jesus' day, the people were sorted into four groups, each of which had different approaches to practical ethics. The general population, the largest group, essentially maintained the status quo, going along with the dominant way of life, and not raising questions. Next, the accommodationists, the Sadducees, for the sake of survival, adjusted their life-styles to that of the existing political powers. Another group, the preservationists, like the Pharisees, dug in their heels and attempted to practice a purer way of life from an earlier and simpler time. On the fringe were the revolutionaries, or Zealots, who were increasingly frustrated with the inadequacy of the other alternatives and ready to take up arms to achieve a new order. Jesus interacted with each of these groups, but did not align himself with any of them. Instead, he took the best from each of them and—critically and constructively—applied their "ways" to the situation in which he found himself.

In the face of the environmental crisis, the strategic situation seems to be similar. The majority of the population, including the membership of the Christian churches, seem to be solid participants in the present system, asking only how they can maintain and advance their position in the process. Those who are critical and who wish to see things change are divided. Some accommodate, seeking to make the best reforms possible without radically changing the system. Others resist, seeing the need for more radical changes in lifestyles, production, and politics, while stopping short of revolutionary change in the system. And a radical fringe, more and more frustrated, is increasingly alienated and divided by sectarian conflict over how to respond to the situation. A part of this latter group is even ready to engage in violence to protect nature and change the system.

The easiest thing for Christians interested in ecological politics to do would be to opt for one or another of these alternatives. But Christians, following the example of Jesus, have the option to integrate the best features of contemporary movements into a larger and more powerful movement. We can apply Jesus' method of listening, responding, and most of all, forgiving, in an attempt to be environmentally responsible.

The period out of which Jesus emerged saw the demise of small city-states with their relatively communal style of politics replaced by a huge, bureaucratically centralized empire. The old, familiar, more decentralized political structures of the Jewish people, while not completely destroyed, were submerged and attached to the new political entity. Those who could recall the old way of doing things were in despair. In this context, Jesus had to be creative in the realm of politics, building a movement from the margins and dregs of society so effective that the authorities could no longer ignore it. It was a movement that, in only a few hundred years, turned the Roman Empire upside down.

We may well live in a similar period of transition. New political forms are demanded. We live in the midst of large political structures which themselves have been overtaken by the world market and the dynamics of science and high technology. And, despite the presence of admittedly outstanding political figures among us, it is questionable whether the political and bureaucratic structures of an earlier era are sufficient for controlling the interrelated dynamics of these tremendous forces. We are faced, as was Jesus, with the task of seeking a new politics that will effect what needs to be done, and with creating a movement outside the existing power structures of society. Once again, Jesus can be our inspiration and our guide.

Jesus not only lived a profound ecological ethic, but he created a method by which earlier creative solutions to problems could be made effective in new circumstances, and created a political movement to effect these changes. At every relevant point, Jesus adds something essential to a Christian ecopolitical ethic, and to the Christian church in its response to the ecological crisis. Indeed, unless we exhibit a measure of Jesus' commitment, his attention to the issues, his flexibility in dealing with problems, and his creativity in political expression, we will not adequately confront the depth of the ecological crisis before us.

Epilogue

Calvin DeWitt

A crisis of degradation is penetrating earth and enveloping its creatures. Freed from physical and religious constraints and dissatisfied with creation's gifts, an ever increasing human population—its force multiplied by powerful machines, its capacity unleashed by creation-consuming structures—converts more and more of the earth into products to gratify immediate needs and wants, resulting in unwanted byproducts and waste. No longer do people, machines, and structures reap only the fruits of creation; they degrade creation's producers, recyclers, and purifiers—interfering with and destroying their ability to cleanse air and water, to bring forth creatures after their kinds, to replenish the living fabric of the earth. Such degradation, while being described and anticipated in the Scriptures, is not condoned by them.

Creation's degradation originates from human dissatisfaction with creation's fruitfulness. Deeming creation's processes too prolonged, people invent structures to speed them up; judging creation's production as marginal for growing needs, people press creation to get ever more. This dissatisfaction leads people to re-form the biosphere "bigger than life." Creation is reshaped into a vending machine structured to gratify any human desire upon demand. Operation of this machine extinguishes creatures that have no utility, overtaxes earth's capacity for recycling materials, short-circuits biospheric processes of purification and restoration. The operation of this machine runs roughshod over the law by which all creation is ordained. Earth groans, complains, speaks. Human impatience—intolerant of God-given law and dissatisfied with creation's pace and productivity—brings creation's degradation.

This dissatisfaction with the gifts of God and God's good creation obtains the Creator's severe judgement (Gen. 3:16–19; Deut. 11:8–21); so too does the consequent destruction of creation. The Scriptures describe this as sinful rebellion against the Creator; it is rebellion calling for destruction of those who destroy the earth (Rev. 11:18). Patient creation and its patient Creator watch, wait.

The Creator's will and desire is that the earth be fair, that the habitat of people be a garden. Satisfaction with God's gifts is expected from God's creatures, and thus also their grateful praise. As the Creator was pleased and satisfied with creation, repeatedly proclaiming it "good," so too is satisfaction expected of those who image God. As all creatures pour forth praise for God's everflowing blessings, so should we. Satisfied with God's provision, we should find contentment to be our greatest profit—our largest gain in all creation (1 Tim. 6:6–21). Meekly and contentedly we should join all creatures in praising the Creator, Provider, and Reconciler of all things.

But we no longer reside in the garden; we dwell on an earth where God's will has not been done, on an earth increasingly defiled and degraded by us. We alter the earth's energy exchange with the sun, degrade and deforest the land, extinguish thousands of species, pollute water, poison the globe, degrade human beings and cultures. Our earlier questions loom before us: How does the New Testament help us respond to degradation caused by land conversion and habitat destruction? What does it say about species extinctions, land degradation, and the production of wastes and hazards? Does it help us respond to global toxification? Or to the alteration of planetary energy exchange? Does it guide us toward a moral response to human and cultural degradation?

The New Testament's response to such questions is a powerful one of ominous consequence. But it is hardly the one we might have expected. For it is a *single* answer to *all* questions. The New Testament teaches us this: "Seek the kingdom." Moreover, it puts the kingdom in a priority position amidst all others; it teaches, "Let the kingdom be the very first thing you seek!" Thus the questions on creation's degradation with which we began are secondary. For, once seeking the kingdom, these questions fall into place. While retaining their full significance, they become part of a larger whole—of a structure of rightness and integrity.

In advising people to seek the kingdom first, the New Testament addresses each of our questions powerfully. While not giving the specifics of the Old Testament law and prophets (for example, saving threatened species, giving the land its Sabbath rests, not adding house to house, and not polluting the waters), the New Testament provides a truly profound base from which the specifics are derivative. It gives the foundation and the structure that puts all environmental issues and problems into context. It provides the capacity to deal with the creation as a whole, with creation in its integrity.

Building upon the teachings of the Old Testament and its anticipation of a restored land, the New Testament breaks forth with a vision of the kingdom of God. As it does this, it brings to greater brightness and clarity the present and future context of these questions; it identifies Christ as the one through whom all things were made and are held together; it points to Christ as the last Adam who undoes the work of the first and sets about to do what Adam was supposed to do in the first place; and it describes Jesus Christ as the Redeemer whose resurrection is the vindication of the Creator's righteousness.

In the preface, I related a conversation about the kingdom of God. Reformulating Wendell Berry's question to Wes Jackson, we now can ask, "What kind of economy would be comprehensive enough to prevent ruination of creation, and bring about its restoration?" Along with Wes Jackson we reply, "The kingdom of God." Wendell Berry's explanation still holds: "the first principle of the kingdom of God is that it includes everything; in it, the fall of every sparrow is a significant event. . . . Another principle, both ecological and traditional, is that everything in the kingdom of God is joined both to it and everything else that is in it. . . ."[1] In the teaching of Jesus in the New Testament the kingdom of God is the central symbol for the new vision of life in its fullness; it involves personal, social, earthly, and cosmic dimensions of salvation; its earthly and cosmic dimensions of restoration lead directly to an ethic of care for the creation. The kingdom of God is a vision of things as they *ought* to be in the entire cosmos, human and nonhuman; it is an order in which *all things* are in right relationship (Zerbe). It is a creation-affirming alternative to those modern structures that bring the creation to ruination and brokenness. It speaks to all our stated questions and more by asking, Can this degradation persist in the kingdom of God—where integrity and rightness dwell? It speaks powerfully that not only is degradation and brokenness to be prevented and halted, but that all degradations—all things—must be reconciled and made right again.

The New Testament teaches that the restoration of the creation's brokenness has already begun in a real, evident, and substantial way, even though the kingdom, now present with us, will be manifested in its totality and perfection in a new creation (Zerbe). In Christ's resurrection we see the first fruits of a new creation in which *all things* have been made right by the atonement—the good creation has reached the beginning of its final glory. When the same Spirit that raised Christ from the dead dwells in those who follow Jesus (Rom. 8:11), then the righteousness of God becomes an active spiritual power (Rom. 8:10) that counters creation's degradations and brings rightness to a groaning creation (Rom. 8). The rightness of the law, first presented in the Old Testament but now fulfilled in the New (Rom. 8:4), is the state of being at peace with the Creator and in a right relation with the creation. Our justification, that is, our being made right with God, means that in Christ we are restored to Adam's position of steward of the earth on behalf of the Creator (Van Leeuwen). As such we are enabled to join Christ in restoring, caring for, and keeping creation.

The kingdom, both present and future, looks forward to a final vision of salvation, namely, a redeemed community of whole persons within a restored creation. The biblical vision of the kingdom of God calls us to be coworkers with Christ in the redemption and healing of the creation; it is divinely and humanly wrought (Zerbe).

The Scriptures describe those who go their own way as disciples of the first Adam, and those who follow Christ as disciples of the last Adam. Jesus Christ is the creating Logos of God—the Word created all things and through whom all things hold together, suffering with God's creation, on the cross (John 1:1–4; Col. 1:17–18; Heb. 1:1–2). Christ, whose death on the cross has redeemed us, is also the Christ in whom and by whom we are created. Thus when we read, "For God so loved the world [*kosmos*] that he gave his only begotten Son," (John 3:16) we not only think of the Creator's love for people, but also for the cosmos—of Christ's work of reconciling *all things* to himself (Col. 1:20). It is a matter of expressive joy and wonder that the Christ of the cross is the Christ of creation. The cost of creation's degradation for the Creator is the self-giving of God; likewise, the cost of our stewardship is our own self-giving. Living out our salvation means ardent, devoted, and faithful engagement of Christians in the stewardship of our Lord's earth (Wilkinson).

And what is the extent of the kingdom? The reach of Christ's work extends everywhere (Eph. 1:19–23; Col. 1:15–20). The work of the last Adam, Jesus Christ, is as broad as the reach of the damage wrought by the first Adam. The work of Christ impacts all human relationships—those with God, with others, and with the cosmos. The deep and broad impact of Adam's disobedience includes a complex of relationships with God, others, and the cosmos. The total well-being of this complex in the garden turns to brokenness and disintegration through Adam's failure and ultimately to creation's degradation. Paul draws an analogy between the first Adam and Christ, the last Adam, showing Christ's obedient work as the undoing of Adam's disobedience. The New Testament calls us to see redemption as a threefold relationship between God, people, and the cosmos; redemption is our calling to all of them, and not one to the exclusion of the others (Manahan).

How do we know that God will bring in the kingdom? Because Christ's resurrection not only vindicates the Creator's righteousness but creation itself. The atoning death and resurrection of Christ brought about our justification and righteousness (Rom. 4:25)—our restoration to the glory which was originally proper to Adam as the royal steward of creation. Paul's teaching on the resurrection in 1 Corinthians 15 affirms the goodness of the present creation in spite of sin and futility. God will not abolish or abandon this world, but will transform and perfect it as the "new creation." With reference to the "new creation" Paul everywhere assumes both continuity and change. In the present penultimate order, those "in Christ" are equipped by the Spirit to care for the earth and to love their neighbor. But obedience or disobedience in the creation brings God's blessing or wrath via the creation itself (Van Leeuwen).

And how do we get from here to there? From the defilement and pollution of earth to the garden? From the dissatisfactions of the world to the contentment of God's children? From the kingdom of this world to the kingdom of God? The New Testament points us to Jesus, the last Adam, as the one we should follow. The Scriptures call us to be disciples of the last Adam, of the one through whom all things were made, through whom all things hold together, and by whom all things are reconciled. The Scriptures call us to follow Jesus, the one who enlivens the law and makes it serve the life it was intended to serve, incorporating the best of the old in terms of the needs of the present. Jesus said, "I have not come to abolish them [the Law and the Prophets], but to fulfill them" (Matt. 5:17). And only in so doing could he say, "I am the way and the truth and the life" (John 14:6). Jesus lived and gave what the law demanded that others, in their confusion, legalism, and bondage, could not achieve on their own (Visick). And the New Testament invites us to follow Jesus.

And who is this Jesus whose approach and style we should emulate? He is one who demonstrates unique effectiveness in action—criticizing the traditional way of doing things, updating these ways in the context of a new situation, and bringing the treasured insights of the past into a creative and life-giving relationship with the present. He is the one that provides us a new live-giving and life-sustaining model—the model of servanthood. Jesus' servanthood, as well as that of those who follow Jesus, focuses on (1) *the service of God*, primarily expressed in the prophetic attack on the inevitable idolatries of politics, and (2) *the service of God's creation*, especially those parts of it diminished, disrupted, or threatened by irresponsible human action. It is a model that stands in sharp contrast with most of our actions today (Visick).

While the easiest approach in our time of ecological crisis is to support a particular political structure, those who follow Jesus' example of servanthood have the option to integrate the best features of contemporary movements into a large and more powerful movement. Christians can apply Jesus' method of listening, responding, and most of all, forgiving, in the attempt to be responsible in creation. Through it they can creatively build a movement of the meek so effective that no one could long ignore it (Visick).

Today, in the context of a crisis of degradation that penetrates the earth and envelops its creatures, in a time when people not only reap the fruits of creation but even degrade creation's producers, recyclers, and purifiers, a response is needed that once again permits and protects the creation's ability to cleanse its air and water and to replenish its living populations of plants and animals. In the midst of creation's garden—so abundantly yielding blessed fruits, sustainably supporting humankind and all life in its God-declared goodness—the social, economic, and political structures we created have themselves been overtaken by the world market and the dynamics of science and technology. Before us the creatures fall—some diminished, some wiped completely from the face of the Creator's canvas. Before us is the trashed gallery of earth's Maker. People and their structures replace divine creation with human creations, perpetrating an overwhelmingly powerful assault on the fabric of the biosphere.

Today, we are faced with the task of controlling the interrelated dynamics of the tremendous forces we have created. Like Jesus, we are faced with the task of seeking a new structure outside existing power structures that will effect what needs to be done (Visick). We are faced with the challenge of seeking first the kingdom of God. And we are challenged to pray, "Your kingdom come, your will be done, on earth. . . ." (Matt. 6:10).

So where does this book bring us?

To New Testament Christians, this book would advise, "We must so behave on earth that heaven will not be a shock to us!" and, "Do not be numbered among those who destroy the earth!"

To those of the Jewish faith, this book would advise, "Live in creation with the law written upon your hearts, so that everything is done in accord with God's ordinances for redeeming and healing humanity and creation."

To those attracted to the New Age movement as an answer to their quest for spiritual and environmental wholeness, this books shows that the New Testament provides a rich and full alternative, a "new age" about which much has been written and believed over thousands of years—the kingdom of God.

To the secular reader, this book discloses resources of the New Testament—of Christian faith—that affirm what many have suspected: Not only is the environmental crisis a human and religious one, but Christianity has important contributions to make toward the reversal of environmental destruction and establishment of ecological sustainability.

To everyone, it would advise that the New Testament and Christianity have much to contribute to the current reflections on environmental and spiritual awareness that are so prevalent.

Environmental responsibility lies at the center of Christian faith and life, requiring every person who professes Christ to be faithful in their care and keeping of the creation. There *is* a distinctively Christian contribution to environmental stewardship; there *is* an important contribution provided by the New Testament. Churches and denominations need to give very clear witness to their profession of Christ as Redeemer *and* Creator—including the provision of living examples of the consequences of being restored, through Christ, to Adam's position of steward of the earth on behalf of the Creator.

Finally, the New Testament is based upon the Old, which advises us, "I have set before you life and death, blessings and curses" (Deut. 30:19). It then advises, "Now choose life, so that you and your children may live and that you may love the LORD your God, listen to his voice, and hold fast to him" (30:19–20).

Appendix

A Review of Environmental Stewardship

Literature and the New Testament

David S. Wise

This review of the literature on the New Testament and environmental issues began with a check of computerized databases of University Microfilms International's dissertations and *Religion Index*. Two formal bibliographies on the topic were also surveyed, *A Search for Environmental Ethics: An Initial Bibliography*, and one by Fred Van Dyke.[1] Subsequently, these bibliographies were checked further for individual sources such as journal articles. The results of that search comprise a bibliography with more than 700 citations.

The focus of the original search was literature on a biblical, environmental ethic. This included sources in both the Old and New Testament. The majority of these, however, represented Old Testament sources.

This search has shown the marked tendency for those writing on environmental stewardship to turn to the Old Testament. Of the six most significant New Testament sources found, only one is dated after 1972, and that is a single chapter revision of an earlier book by the same author. The others have dates of 1961, 1967, 1970, 1971, and 1972.[2]

The Fulfillment of Creation in the New Testament

The Renewal of Creation: A Minority Viewpoint?

Is the final aim of God, in his governance of all things, to bring into being at the very end a glorified kingdom of spirits alone who, thus united with God, may contemplate him in perfect bliss, while as a precondition of their ecstasy all the other creatures of nature must be left by God to fall away into eternal oblivion?

Or is the final aim of God, in his governance of all things, to communicate his life to another in a way which calls forth at the very end new heavens and a new earth in which righteousness dwells, a transfigured cosmos where peace is universally established between all creatures at last, in the midst of which is situated a glorious city of resurrected saints who dwell in justice, blessed with all the resplendent fullness of the earth, and who continually call upon all creatures to join with them in their joyful praise of the one who is all in all?[3]

In this question, H. Paul Santmire identifies two primary streams of interpretation of what the Scriptures say regarding the future of creation. The first option envisions the salvation of human souls alone, with nonhuman creation "falling away into eternal oblivion." The second sees resurrected humans and all creation fulfilled, joyfully praising God.

Of the two readings of Scripture, Louis Taylor reports the first as being more widely held in Christian theology.[4] This view regards the grace won through Christ's atoning death as applying only to humans. The following words of Gordon Kaufman are widely cited as representative.

The great words of the Christian vocabulary—sin, salvation, forgiveness, repentance, hope, faith, love, righteousness—have to do primarily with man and with man's relation to God and to his fellows, and the principal conceptual work of Christian theology has been devoted to elaboration of profound interpretations of man's nature and predicament and of the idea of God. The rest of creation, though always recognized and sometimes acknowledged and even reflected upon, simply was not of central theological interest or importance, and (with the exception of angels) never became the subject of any technical theological vocabulary or doctrines.[5]

Despite Taylor's statement, an overwhelming majority of the sources consulted support the view that all of creation is intended for ultimate renewal. Whether this observation is due to the way sources were selected or due to a change over time in the consensus of the theological community is unclear.[6]

In all, over twenty-five writers provide support (either explicit or implicit) for a cosmic renewal.[7] The statements of the two following authors epitomize this finding.

George H. Williams states that

> in Christian eschatology there has been place not only for the immortality of the soul but also for the resurrection of the flesh and a place also in the inauguration of the kingdom of God for the purification of all creation to be redeemed for a new heaven and for a new earth.[8]

The Renewal of Creation as the Fulfillment of God's Intentions

The future renewal of creation may also be viewed as the fulfillment of God's intentions for it. Hugh Montefiore expresses this idea.

> The Christian view of history involves the concept of purpose and design. Saint Paul looks forward to the time when God will be "all in all." Revelation looks forward to the new creation, a new heaven and a new earth. All will be recapitulated. Nothing will be wasted. Redemption is, in Christian theology, to be extended to the whole divine purpose for the world of nature, bringing to birth new possibilities at present unknown and enabling the whole world to reach the fulfillment of its potentialities.[9]

This expectation of final fulfillment can be traced through both testaments. Bernhard W. Anderson sees the author of Genesis pointing from creation to a new beginning after the flood, with an ultimate Sabbath rest as a final goal.[10] Isaiah echoes this theme, presenting God as the First, who laid earth's foundations, and the Last, who will bring about the new heavens and the new earth. Similar thinking, the coming transformation of the world, can be seen in Christ's teaching.[11] Paul speaks of the day when creation itself will be set free from its bondage to decay and will be brought into liberty. Finally, in symmetry with Genesis' words "In the beginning God," Revelation speaks of God as, in the end, ushering in the new heavens and the new earth.[12] God's work of redemption is symmetrical in purpose and scale to his work of creation.

New Testament Anticipation of a Renewed Creation

The New Testament view of creation's future stands in continuity with the view of the Old Testament. The future renewal of all creation is a theme which persists throughout the Old Testament. Writers find support from the first book, Genesis, to the next-to-last, Zechariah. Citing Genesis 49:11 and Numbers 24:5–7 in his significant thesis, Kenneth Maahs states, "one of the most persistent features of this anticipated future is the hope for a transformed and glorified natural environment."[13] In Cox's view, the words of Isaiah 55:12–13 and 65:17 give classic expression to the thought:

> You will go out in joy
>   and be led forth in peace;
> the mountains and hills
>   will burst into song before you,
> and all the trees of the field
>   will clap their hands.
> Instead of thornbush will grow the pine tree,
>   and instead of briers the myrtle will grow.
> This will be for the LORD's renown,
>   for an everlasting sign,
>   which will not be destroyed.
>
> (55:12–13)
>
> Behold, I will create
> new heavens and a new earth.[14]
>
> (65:17)

Cox states that the discussion of nonhuman creation in the New Testament, though limited in quantity and detail, has continuity with the more full presentations found in the Old Testament. Indeed, the New Testament assumes them. While the New Testament is not as explicit, it does reflect the Old Testament's expectation of a comprehensive restoration.

For example, at first it appears lamentable that Paul's reference in Romans 8 to the renewal of creation is so brief and incidental. However, it is quite significant that Paul, as laborious and careful as he is to develop his writing fully, mentions the idea in a rather indirect fashion. His very manner reveals that for him (and arguably, for his audience) the future redemption of creation was sufficiently common an expectation to merit no further attention. Indeed, Paul's earlier life as Saul the Pharisee would have insured his thorough familiarity with the Old Testament.[15]

Lindeskog suggests that the notion of creation's restoration developed in the theological climate of the intertestamental period, which later influenced Paul's mind-set and assumptions. He states that in the view of the writings of that period, "there will be a future when God will redeem His creation."[16] He adds, "this literature forms a useful commentary on the Old Testament, and indicates the teachings about creation which were current in our Lord's day. The development of eschatology is the most important feature of post-canonical Jewish literature, and its most fruitful teaching was the idea of the new creation."[17]

A number of other New Testament sources support the expectation of a cosmic renewal. Discussion begins with the teachings of Christ. Santmire speaks of Christ's self-understanding as recorded in the Gospels.

> The coming of the Final Day is a central theme in the teaching of Jesus. Study of the "parables of growth" shows that he conceived of the Kingdom of God as coming in two stages, first, in his own words and works, second, in a final world-consummation. This final day, as Jesus depicted it, would be not just the end of the world ("heaven and earth shall pass away"), but the coming of a new world (*palingenesia*).[18]

How Christ was understood by his disciples and later followers reinforce such a view of Christ's teachings. From words such as those in Mark 4:35–41 (Christ's calming of the sea), 2 Corinthians

5:17 ("Therefore, if anyone is in Christ, he is a new creation; the old has gone, the new has come!"), and Romans 5:12–20 (Christ as the second Adam), Santmire sees the incarnation as a new creation. Especially when coupled with the resurrection, this "new creation" can be seen as a a foretaste or a model of the coming transformation that will include the whole creation.

Santmire sees further New Testament support in Luke's Gospel, the Book of Acts, and 2 Peter, all of which hold to the apocalyptic vision of a "new heaven and a new earth, the home of righteousness" (2 Pet. 3:13).[19] But the key text for a discussion of creation's future renewal is Paul's writing in Romans 8, to which our discussion now turns.

Santmire cites J. Christian Beker's reference to Romans 8 as "a key to understanding the whole of Paul's theology."[20] Santmire agrees with the apparent majority of sources consulted when he says,

> here Paul speaks about the groaning of the whole creation and thereby anticipates the day of the new heavens and the new earth, familiar in apocalyptic expectation. This interpretation of Romans 8 is to be contrasted with the assumptions of the anthropocentric view of the biblical theology of nature: that the travail of creation envisioned in Romans 8 either refers chiefly to human history (Bultmann, Barth) or it is some flight of poetic fancy, related obscurely to the fact that humans have a body which is to be redeemed (Lampe).[21]

A paraphrase of Romans 8:19–23 by Paulos M. Gregorios represents the view of the majority of the sources encountered in this writer's search of the literature.

> For the created order awaits, with eager longing, with neck outstretched, the full manifestation of the children of God. The futility or emptiness to which the created order is now subject is not something intrinsic to it. The Creator made the creation contingent, in his ordering, upon hope; for the creation itself has something to look forward to—namely, to be freed from its present enslavement to disintegration. The creation itself is to share in the freedom, in the glorious and undying goodness, of the children of God. For we know how the whole creation up till now has been groaning together in agony, in a common pain. And not just the nonhuman created order—even we ourselves, as Christians, who have received the advance gift of the Holy Spirit, are

now groaning within ourselves, for we are also waiting—waiting for the transformation of our bodies and for the full experiencing of our adoption as God's children.[22]

Gregorios adds, "Human redemption can be understood only as an integral part of the redemption of the whole creation."[23] John Gibbs concludes that

if "the creation" may be taken to mean the entire creation [which Gibbs does], then, Paul says two things about this creation: first, that there is a solidarity between man and creation so that creation is affected by man's action; and, second, that in its very creatureliness creation is a recipient of God's grace "in hope."[24]

Characteristics of the Renewed Creation

As the discussion now turns to consider the specific attributes of the renewed creation, the sheer limits of human understanding and language must be recognized. Santmire's thinking will provide the outline for this section, and his first thoughts highlight the limits which must be noted.

Yet as we enter this province we should recognize that our theological language must remain, when all has been said, the language of prayer. It is salutary to recall here the traditional saying, *omnium exeunt in mysterium*, we see, but we see through a glass darkly. We can say very little about the new creation which is more than tentative. The fact that the tree of theological reflection is not a mighty oak but a tender vine is especially evident in the present context.[25]

Having said this, Santmire then offers two affirmations about the nature of the new creation. First, the new creation will show significant continuity with the present creation, although it will undergo important transformation. Second, the present creation's "dark side," its chaotic elements, will disappear.[26]

Continuity Between the First and Coming Creations

Considering more fully the continuity of the future with the present creation, Santmire writes the following:

The new creation will stand in a relation of *continuity* with the first creation. The creative rule of God will not destroy the first creation and establish something entirely different. That would be no fulfillment. "For the substance of the creation is not annihilated, since he who established it is faithful. Rather the form of the world passes away," said Irenaeus.[27]

He notes, however, that this continuity does not mean sameness. The coming creation will transcend the present (2 Pet. 3:12–13). John Reumann speaks more strongly than Santmire of the coming creation's likeness to the Garden of Eden. While he notes the dissimilarity of the present and future creations, he concludes from the last verse of Isaiah (esp. 65:17–25) that the future creation is a return to Eden. There the language alludes to Isaiah 11:6–9, which speaks of the return of peace among all creatures, even predator and prey. He maintains that

> the great time to come when Yahweh changes things will be like the golden age of creation when he first made the world (in a famous formula, *"Endzeit gleicht Urzeit,"* eschatology will recapitulate protology).[28]

With this, Lindeskog concurs.

> The eschatology of later prophecy looked further, to a final end when the old world would end in total catastrophe before the creation of a new heaven and a new earth. This new creation would be the restoration of the original state of creation as it was before the Fall.[29]

Elaborating on the transcendent quality of the new creation, Santmire notes strong continuity, but "the new creation will stand in a relation o: *radical transcendence* to the first. The Last Day of the Divine Rest will not be 'more of the same.' "

Reumann's discussion of Isaiah 65:17 corresponds to this motif. This text is the first place that the phrase "new heavens and a new earth" appears in the Bible. Reumann notes with interest the writer's choice of the Hebrew verb *bārā* for the act of creating. This verb form is precisely the one used by the author of Genesis throughout chapters 1 and 2 to describe God's creative activity. Due to the choice of this particular verb by the author of Isaiah, Reumann maintains that Isaiah implies that the creative activity of God in bringing about the new heavens and earth will be comparable with the initial act of creation. The extent of change will be so great that it will appear as a totally new act of creation; this speaks of a transcendent new creation.[30]

Louis Taylor preceded Reumann in describing the extent of transformation to occur in the new creation. Taylor sees this aspect of Christian eschatology as following the lines of Jewish eschatology of the intertestamental period. He cites 2 Esdras 4:27ff. as illustrating his point.

> This age is full of sadness and infirmities. For the evil about which you asked me has been sown. If therefore that which has been sown is not reaped, and if the place where the evil has been sown does not pass away, the field where the good has been sown will not come. In other words, it is not enough to pluck out the weeds which keep springing up in the soil of the present world. The transformation must be more radical and far reaching. The whole soil which inevitably goes on producing these weeds must be done away with. The whole field, in which the germs of the weed seeds lie dormant, must disappear, and a completely new field must take its place. To drop the metaphors, it is not enough to fill this ground-form of world history, time, with a new content, so that the time of disaster and struggle is succeeded by a time of happiness and world peace. No, the whole form of temporality must be abolished. This new world form—this is the decisive conviction of the late apocalyptists—exists altogether beyond the whole of our present imagination.[31]

Taylor concludes that

> the whole fantastic idea of a golden age of the world, the picture of an idealized, gigantically magnificent humanity in the midst of a natural paradise has suddenly and utterly vanished in the New Testament. Instead there appears something altogether different, something which cannot be expressed positively, but only negatively: "an inheritance which is imperishable, undefiled, and unfading" (1 Peter 1:4). Paul says: "For this perishable nature must put on the imperishable, and this mortal nature must put on immortality. When the perishable puts on the imperishable, and the mortal puts on immortality, then shall come to pass the saying that is written: "Death is swallowed up in victory.""[32]

Taylor reads Paul's word "the creation itself will be liberated from its bondage to decay" (Rom. 8:21) precisely through these glasses, and envisions a new creation that greatly transcends the present one. Thus the discussion encloses unavoidable ambiguity with the tension between Santmire's themes of continuity and transcendence.

The End of Creation's "Dark Side"

Another characteristic of the new creation will be the end of the first creation's "dark side." Santmire roughly traces the outlines of this thought:

> All the chaotic elements of nature will be put to rest. This seems to be the meaning of the Apocalypse's affirmation that the sea will be no more (Rev. 21:1). The natural pain and death of the first creation will thereby be overcome (Rev. 21:4). So too, aggression and conflict of the first creation will vanish in the "peaceable kingdom."[33]

In this statement, Santmire identifies the two major elements also noted by others—the peaceable kingdom and the victory over death.

Kenneth Maahs identifies the future peace of creation as one of the most prominent themes in biblical eschatology. Its meaning goes far beyond the absence of aggression to imply the fullest manifestation of life as God intends it.

> *Shalom* (peace) is God's dream and promise for the fulfillment of his creation . . . the knitting together of all the brokenness in the cosmos, in the relations between man and man, a man and himself, man and nature, within nature, and between man-nature and God.[34]

This image of peace is the peace of the original creation. Much of the prophetic image of the coming creation speaks of peace understood in these terms—all creatures dwelling together without violence. Isaiah 11 contains this image. To Maahs's thinking, Hosea shares this same vision as he describes the covenant God will make with the creatures (Hos. 4:18). This understanding of the peace that is to come in the new creation occurs through the transformation of the creatures

Maahs also notes that Leviticus 26:6 points to a future time of peace achieved through the removal of wild animals. He sees both Isaiah 35:9 and Ezekiel 34:25 as building on this text in Leviticus. These two prophetic texts describe a future free from animal attacks due to their removal from the land. Maahs does not find any resolution to these two divergent streams of thought—the *presence* of peaceful animals and the *absence* of violent animals. Yet he feels that he can conclude that "their meaning is essentially the same. The animal world will again know a unity founded on covenantal brotherhood."[35]

Finally, the discussion turns to consider the new creation's victory over death. Opinions differ on the specific meaning of the Scriptures and it seems that the Scriptures themselves present varying viewpoints. Taylor speaks with confidence that death, as known in this creation, will be done away with in the coming creation.

> This abolition of the present world form will show itself negatively in that the rigid, fundamental law, to which all life in the present world is subject . . . will be cancelled—the biological principle that life can only increase and multiply by a process in which other life is suffocated and destroyed with pain and deadly torture. This abolition of the present law of life is implicit in the promise: "He will wipe away every tear from their eyes and death shall be no more, neither shall there be mourning nor crying nor pain any more, for the former things have passed away" (Revelation 21:4).[36]

Working with an apocalyptic text in Isaiah 65, Reumann finds another view of the change in death brought by the new creation. Here God himself speaks of new heavens and a new earth that he will create (65:20).

> Never again will there be in it
>   an infant who lives but a few days,
>   or an old man who does not live out his years;
> he who dies at a hundred
>   will be thought a mere youth;
> he who fails to reach a hundred
>   will be considered accursed.

In these verses, Reumann reads a promise that *premature* death will not be a part of the new creation, but he does not see these verses as totally ruling out death as Taylor infers from Revelation 21.

Santmire goes even further as he questions whether death, disease, and physical suffering have an appropriate place in the present creation.

> Even to raise this question is to stand at a certain distance from the main line of theological tradition, for many theologians have assumed or explicitly taught that physical death is the result of sin. Nevertheless it is possible to contend that both death and suffering belong in some sense to the world as created. Such modern theologians as Reinhold Niebuhr, Paul Althaus, and Karl Barth have argued persuasively in this vein. The theology of the Bible generally seems to move in the same direction, providing little support for the alternative view that physical death and suffering are the result of a cosmic fall.[37]

Given Santmire's thoughts about the place of death in the *present* creation it is difficult and perhaps even misleading to extrapolate his views on the place of death in the *coming* creation. The wider consensus among writers seems clear, however, that in the coming creation, death will have an altered significance and may disappear altogether.

The Meaning of Righteousness in the New Testament

A discussion of righteousness in the New Testament begins by examining the Old Testament background, which the New Testament basically assumes. On this, Schmid suggests that

> the basic theme of ancient Near Eastern views of creation was the question about the orderly (*heil*) world, the question of a comprehensive righteousness according to the presuppositions of the time. This is precisely the theme of the Bible too, both in the OT and the NT—not the least under the catchword "righteousness." This thematic congruence is not accidental but arises necessarily from the fact that the message of the Bible touches people in their world and in the fundamental questions of human existence.[38]

J. A. Ziesler undertakes the task of thoroughly examining the meaning of righteousness in Paul's writings. Notably, he begins with a study of its use in the Old Testament. There, Ziesler laboriously examines each of the 481 occurrences of the words ṣedeq, ṣĕdāqâ, and ṣaddîq. The primary question he brings to the task is whether these words connote "forensic" or "ethical/relational" aspects of righteousness. By "forensic righteousness," he means innocence of charges as before a judge—not being guilty. The other meaning of righteousness has to do with acting properly in one's relationships in the world in the larger context of a relationship with God. The difference is not immediately clear, but involves the distinction between *innocence before a judge* and *proper relationships*. The first meaning might be seen as moral, the second more as ecological in scope. Ziesler observes that over 90 percent of the uses of "righteousness" in the Old Testament refer to the second meaning—that of *proper relationships*. He argues that

> most scholars regard righteousness as fundamentally concerned with relationships . . . it is generally agreed that righteousness is behaviour proper to some relationship.[39]

Ziesler's work on the Old Testament meaning of righteousness serves as valuable background for the New Testament usage of the term, to which we now turn. Ziesler interprets Galatians and Romans as providing the clearest understanding of Paul's use of the term. The Book of Romans itself contains twenty-one noun and adjective forms and an additional forty-two cognates. According to Zeisler, the specific understanding of righteousness in the New Testament follows denominational lines. He asks, "Is the Christian made righteous by Christ, and if so what does 'righteous' mean? Or is he declared righteous, i.e. acquitted or brought into a right relationship?"[40] Answering his own question, he suggests that

> the traditional Roman Catholic view is that of the Council of Trent, that justification is both an acquittal and a making righteous in the full ethical sense, thus embracing both relational and behavioural renewal. It means the sinner's forgiveness *and* his moral regeneration, i.e. his sanctification.[41]

Such an understanding rests on several lines of thought. First, the word used, *dikaioō*, is interpreted as "to make righteous" in an ethical sense. Second, noun forms of the word receive greater emphasis than verb forms. The result is that in passages like 1 Corinthians 1:30 and 2 Corinthians 5:21 the noun interprets the verb. Third, God's word of justification is seen as a creative word. If God *declares* someone righteous, they are indeed made righteous. Fourth, as forgiveness is connected with the cross, justification is connected with the resurrection, which brings new life in its entirety. Fifth, when one is justified and in Christ, one is a new creature, as in the image of baptism. Overall then, the process of justification leads to righteous understood as sanctification.[42]

In contrast to the Catholic view, Protestant interpretation emphasizes the verbal form of the word, that is, "to make righteous." The Protestant view holds that the verb declares the believer righteous—a matter of status only. On linguistic grounds alone, Ziesler sees this view as more defensible than the Catholic view. Yet in spite of this, Protestants vary in their understanding. While some of them view justification as mere acquittal, others see it as restoration to right relationship. Ziesler reiterates this second view: "Others see the forensic dress as subsidiary and relatively unimportant; what matters is that *justify* means *to restore to right relationship*."[43]

Thus, except for those Protestants who regard justification as a matter of acquittal rather than restoration in a relationship, the New Testament understanding of righteousness stands in direct continuity with the Old Testament.

The Final Restoration of Righteousness According to 2 Peter

In 2 Peter 3 the reader can see the hope of a final restoration of the earth that will conform to God's intended righteousness. The author envisions that "in keeping with his promise we are looking forward to a new heaven and a new earth, the home of righteousness" (2 Pet. 3:13).

Earlier verses in 2 Peter 3 seem to indicate that God's refining fire will be the mechanism that brings "a new heaven and a new earth, the home of righteousness."

The heavens will disappear with a roar; the elements will be destroyed by fire, and the earth and everything in it will be laid bare. Since everything will be destroyed in this way, what kind of people ought you to be? You ought to live holy and godly lives as you look forward to the day of God and speed its coming. That day will bring about the destruction of the heavens by fire, and the elements will melt in the heat.[44]

Fire is an image used widely throughout Scriptures, drawing on the analogy of the refinement of metals. Contaminants in precious metals, called dross, are removed in a process using fire to heat the metal to its melting point. Reference to precious metals (as opposed to iron or bronze) emphasizes the value to the metallurgist of the noncorrupt portion. In Scripture, the pure metal is the righteous portion of God's creation, while the dross is the unrighteous portion. Thus the image of fire refers not so much to total destruction as to purification by the removal of contaminating elements—typically, human sinfulness or sinners. Examples are numerous, but a few will suffice. The first shows in a negative way the image of fire as a purifying, rather than destructive, agent. The LORD says,

the house of Israel has become dross to me; all of them are the copper, tin, iron and lead left inside a furnace. They are but the dross of silver. . . . I will gather you and I will blow on you with my fiery wrath, and you will be melted. . . . and you will know that I the LORD have poured out my wrath upon you.[45]

In this case the image of fire is, atypically, one of destruction: "Typically, imagery used by others to represent purifying was used by Ezekiel to picture total destruction."[46]

Texts from Isaiah and Malachi represent the wider Old Testament usage.

See how the faithful city
     has become a harlot!
She once was full of justice;
     righteousness used to dwell in her—
     but now murderers!
Your silver has become dross,
     your choice wine is diluted with water.

> I will turn my hand against you;
> > I will thoroughly purge away your dross
> > and remove all your impurities.
>
> . . . .
>
> Afterward you will be called
> > the City of Righteousness,
> > the Faithful City.[47]

But who can endure the day of his coming? Who can stand when he appears? For he will be like a refiner's fire or a launderer's soap. He will sit as a refiner and purifier of silver; he will purify the Levites and refine them like gold and silver. Then the LORD will have men who bring offerings in righteousness.[48]

The New Testament use is similar, using fire to destroy the contaminating elements of sin and sinners. In Matthew's Gospel, Jesus says,

As the weeds are pulled up and burned in the fire, so it will be at the end of the age. The Son of Man will send out his angels, and they will weed out of his kingdom everything that causes sin and all who do evil. They will throw them into the fiery furnace, where there will be weeping and gnashing of teeth. Then the righteous will shine like the sun in the kingdom of their Father.[49]

In the Book of Revelation the Alpha and Omega, the Lord God (see Rev. 1:8), says,

He who overcomes will inherit all this, and I will be his God and he will be my son. But the cowardly, the unbelieving, the vile, the murderers, the sexually immoral, those who practice magic arts, the idolaters and all liars—their place will be in the fiery lake of burning sulfur.[50]

Our discussion returns again to the text of 2 Peter 3:10–12. Do the words about a fiery destruction refer to the total annihilation of creation? Second Peter 3:6 consciously refers to the creation as already having been "destroyed" by the flood of Genesis, yet the physical planet continues to exist. The purpose of the "destruction" of the earth in the flood was regenerative. It destroyed the discordant element in creation—wicked humans beings[51]—and restored the righteousness intended by God for creation. The coming destruction anticipated by 2 Peter can be understood similarly using the image of purification by fire. Significantly, the aforementioned passages in Isaiah 1 and 2 Peter 3 share the image of righteousness "dwelling" in the newly purified realm, as in a "home."

The destruction of sin and/or sinners is shown as a necessary precondition of the restoration of righteousness. This is the testimony of the Genesis flood narrative and a peculiar phrase in Psalm 104. The psalmist has just finished a beautiful poetic retelling of God's actions in creating and sustaining a world of righteousness in the fullest, ecological sense of the word. As he concludes, he asks God's acceptance of his praise. Just before two closing items of praise, he includes a phrase that at first seems utterly foreign to the entire psalm. He adds, "But may sinners vanish from the earth and the wicked be no more" (Ps. 104:35). Such a rapid shift in tone is striking and seems inconsistent. But for the psalmist, such a wish is completely consistent with the tenor of the poem; surely no human should destroy the rich fullness of God's creation, which God so carefully made and maintains. In his request that the wicked perish, the psalmist acknowledges that humans are responsible for the brokenness of creation. Additional commentary helps clarify matters further.

> The psalmist prays for the restoration of the original, intended harmony of creation. Ancient Hebrew man tended to use the personal and concrete words (*sinners . . . wicked*) where we should use the impersonal and abstract ("sin," "wickedness").[52]

The idea of sin and/or sinners opposing righteousness also relates directly to the image of the refining fire. Psalm 119:119 says, "All the wicked of the earth you discard like dross." Proverbs 25:4–5 says, "Remove the dross from the silver, and out comes material for the silversmith; remove the wicked from the king's presence, and his throne will be established through righteousness." Both passages compare wicked humans to dross and show them opposing righteousness.

In the light of the preceding discussion, it is possible to ascertain from 2 Peter a vision of a coming renewal of creation. The heavens and the earth will indeed be plunged into a consuming fire, but it will be a *refiner's* fire. The outcome is not the annihilation of creation, but rather its cleansing—the removal of the dross of sin and sinners. The creation that emerges from the crucible will be a purified one, fit to be called "the home of righteousness." On this point, Paul Evdokimov concurs.

> The image of the eschatological fire (2 Peter 3:10) is a transcendent symbol. It situates the metamorphosis beyond history (Revelation 21:24). But the whole body of texts of this type shows that it is not a question of destruction, pure and simple, of nature, but of nature's passage through the trial of fire which purifies and preserves all that withstands the flame, just as formerly Noah's Ark was saved through the trial of the waters. It is not a new "Hexaemeron," but the renewal of the existing: a new Earth. God has willed it so. His kingdom is not a transplantation foreign to the being of the world, but the revelation of the world's hidden noumenal depth.[53]

Thus do a number of contemporary works treat the question of the relationship between Christianity and the environment. If this sampling accurately reflects a general trend, then it seems that serious theological reflection on this topic is increasing and that work of this nature will be abundant in years to come.

About the Contributors

Calvin B. DeWitt is professor of environmental studies at the Institute for Environmental Studies at the University of Wisconsin-Madison. He is also director of the Au Sable Institute of Environmental Studies in Mancelona, Michigan. For a decade he has been leading this Institute into new inquiries concerning the meaning of Christian faith for environmental stewardship. A contributor to *Earthkeeping: Christian Stewardship of Natural Resources*, he has written and lectured widely on the environment, stewardship, and religious ethics. Dr. DeWitt earned his B.A. from Calvin College, and his graduate degrees in biology from the University of Michigan. Prior to coming to Wisconsin, he was a professor of biology at the University of Michigan in Dearborn.

Raymond C. Van Leeuwen is associate professor of Old Testament at Calvin College and Seminary, where he has taught since 1981. After receiving a degree in classical languages from Calvin College, he studied Semitic languages, Scripture, and theology at the University of Toronto, where he earned the Ph.D. degree in 1984. Scholars Press published his *Context and Meaning in Proverbs 25–27* in 1988. Growing up in the smog of Los Angeles, Dr. Van Leeuwen became convinced early on that something was wrong in the relationship between humans and nature.

Ronald Manahan is vice president for College Academic Affairs at Grace College, Winona Lake, Indiana. Growing up in a evangelical and pietistic church background, he graduated from Grand Rapids School of the Bible and Music, Shelton College, and Grace Theological Seminary. He also studied at Calvin Theological Seminary and Union Theological Seminary (Virginia). Dr. Manahan has come to see stewardship as growing out of the redeeming work of Christ, and as related to the whole of creation.

Vernon Visick serves the University of Wisconsin-Madison as campus minister for Madison Campus Ministry. He is also a Ph.D. candidate at the Divinity School of the University of Chicago in the field of ethics and society. After graduating from Whitworth College in Spokane, Washington, he received his ministerial training at the Evangelical Theological Seminary in Naperville, Illinois, He is the coeditor of *God and Capitalism*, a new volume of essays that deals with the religious interpretation of economics.

Loren Wilkinson is professor of philosophy and integrative studies at Regent College, a graduate school of theology at the University of British Columbia in Vancouver. He has also taught at Trinity College, Seattle Pacific University, Calvin College, and in the Oregon Extension. The editor of *Earthkeeping: Christian Stewardship of Natural Resources*, he has written and lectured extensively on issues concerning the human use of creation. He has graduate degrees in writing and modern literature from Johns Hopkins, philosophy of religion from Trinity Evangelical Divinity School, and a doctorate in humanities from Syracuse University.

David Wise is currently a graduate student in land resources at the University of Wisconsin-Madison, writing a thesis entitled "A Biblical Land Ethic." He recently joined the faculty at Lancaster Mennonite High School in Pennsylvania where he designed and teaches a course that integrates the study of environmental issues with concepts of biblical stewardship. With his wife, Sally, he lives on the school's 100-acre campus where they are "stewards in residence," planting trees, stopping creek bank erosion, and doing other environmentally useful tasks. He earned his B.S. degree at Pennsylvania State University in environmental resource management. Prior to graduate study, he worked with the Soil Bioengineering Corporation of Marietta, Georgia, where he helped design erosion control plans using native vegetation He also worked with the Pennsylvania Department of Environmental Resources in their scenic rivers program.

Endnotes

Preface

1. Wendell Berry, *Home Economics* (San Francisco: North Point Press, 1987), 44.

Introduction

1. See Wesley Granberg-Michaelson, ed., *Tending the Garden* (Grand Rapids: Eerdmans, 1987), and Loren Wilkinson, ed., *Earthkeeping: Christian Stewardship of Natural Resources* (Grand Rapids: Eerdmans, 1980).

2. Isaiah 5:8.
3. Genesis 6:19.
4. Leviticus 25:1; 26:14, 32, 35.
5. Ezekiel 34:18.
6. Jeremiah 2:7.
7. Deuteronomy 32:6.
8. Leviticus 25:17, 23, 28.
9. Jeremiah 8:7.
10. Isaiah 24:4–5.
11. Deuteronomy 30:19–20.

Chapter 1

1. Paulos M. Gregorios, "New Testament Foundations for Understanding the Creation," in Wesley Granberg-Michaelson, *Tending the Garden* (Grand Rapids: Eerdmans, 1987), 90.

2. For a fuller discussion of these roots of the Johannine use of *logos*, see Loren Wilkinson, "Cosmic Christology and the Christian's Role in Creation," *Christian Scholar's Review* 11 (1981): 18–40.

3. Since it is widely accepted that the Epistle to the Hebrews originated in the widespread community of Hellenized Jews, the very absence of *logos* terminology is significant. One wonders if the term was not almost too ready-to-hand for the syncretistic tendencies of the day, much as the term "cosmic Christ" is today. But that is speculation.

4. Gregorios, "New Testament Foundations," 87–88.

5. This picture of the creating Spirit of God renewing the face of the earth seems to echo the first reference in the Bible to the Spirit of God (Gen. 1:2) which the NIV translates: "the spirit of God was hovering over the waters." There is some debate over whether this refers indeed to the creative moving of God's Spirit, or is instead simply the "wind of God," stirring up the formlessness described in the first part of verse 2. (For a good discussion of this issue, see Claus Westermann, *Genesis 1–11: A Commentary*, trans. John J. Scullion [Minneapolis: Augsburg, 1984], 107–08.) Here the fact that Heb. *rûaḥ* (like Gk. *pneuma*) can mean either "wind" or "spirit" makes it difficult to draw a definite conclusion. The strong parallel to Psalm 104:30, which links the Spirit to the renewing of the face of the earth, would seem to support the opinion that this is a beginning of God's creative action. But there is a sense in which this

confusion between *rûaḥ* as "spirit" and "wind" supports the argument that God is radically immanent in creation. Insomuch as language is possible at all—and surely language is an evidence in humanity of God's image—it is only possible as human beings reach into the creation and use "things" from the immanence of their own involvement in the word to embody their own transcendent meaning. See Owen Barfield, "Philology and the Incarnation," in *The Rediscovery of Meaning* (Middleton, Conn.:Wesleyan University Press, 1977).

6. Jürgen Moltmann, *God in Creation: A New Theology of Creation and the Spirit of God* (San Francisco: Harper and Row, 1985), 14.

7. Moltmann, *God in Creation*, 14.

8. Romans 3:25.

9. For example, Isaiah 65:17, which says, "Behold, I will create new heavens and a new earth."

10. Irenaeus, *Against Heresies*, V, xviii.3, ed. Alexander Roberts and James Donaldson, in *The Ante-Nicene Fathers* (1885; reprint, Grand Rapids: Eerdmans, 1979), 1:546–47.

11. St. Athanasius, *On the Incarnation* (Crestwood, N.Y.: St. Vladimirs Press, n.d.), 26.

12. Ibid., 33–34

13. Frederick W. Dillistone, *The Christian Understanding of Atonement* (Welwyn: James Nisbet & Co., 1968), 406.

14. Vladimir Lossky, *The Mystical Theology of the Eastern Church* (London: James Clark & Co., 1957), 111.

15. Dietrich Bonhoeffer, *The Cost of Discipleship* (New York: Macmillan, 1963), 99.

16. Charles Williams, "The Meaning of the Cross," in *The Image of the City*. (Oxford: Oxford University Press, 1958), 136.

Chapter 2

1. D. E. H. Whitely, *The Theology of St. Paul* (Oxford: Basil Blackwell, 1964), 45. He said that this solidarity makes clear enough that "our involvement in sin and death and our salvation through Christ depend upon

our being in some sense 'one with' both the first man, Adam, and the last Adam."

2. H. W. Robinson, *Corporate Personality in Ancient Israel* (Philadelphia: Fortress, 1964), 1. Several other scholars, including J. A. T. Robinson (*The Body* [London: SCM, 1952]) and A. R. Johnson (*The Vitality of the Individual in the Thought of Ancient Israel* [Cardiff: University of Wales Press, 1964]), have followed Robinson's early lead on the idea, which he first expressed in a German edition published in 1936. Through the years H. W. Robinson's first observations have proven very fruitful. However, recent interpreters have pointed out errors in judgment of those who have overzealously applied the concept of corporate personality. Caution is appropriate.

3. Note the use of Gk. *hōsper*, "just like," in 1 Corinthians 15:22.

4. The "protasis" is the opening proposition of a rational syllogism, the closing statement of which is the "apodosis."

5. C. C. Caragounis, "Romans 5.15–16 in the Context of 5.12–21: Contrast or Comparison?" *New Testament Studies* 31 (1985): 143.

6. See note 4 above.

7. Caragounis, "Romans 5.15–16," 144–46.

8. Ibid., 146.

9. Elsewhere I have spelled out this relational existence of human beings in some detail. See R. E. Manahan, "A Reexamination of the Cultural Mandate: An Analysis and Evaluation of the Dominion Materials" (Th.D. diss., Grace Theological Seminary, 1982), 116–32. This thesis provides a fuller treatment of many of the motifs in this paper. Abraham Kuyper had noted these three relationships during his 1898 Stone Lectures at Princeton Seminary. See Abraham Kuyper, *Lectures on Calvinism* (Grand Rapids: Eerdmans, 1931), 9–40.

10. On "image" (*ṣelem*), compare Numbers 33:52; 1 Samuel 6:5 (twice), 11; 2 Kings 11:18; 2 Chronicles 23:17: Ezekiel 7:20; 16:17; 23:14; and Amos 5:26. Though the uses occurring in Psalms 39:6 (MT 7) and 73:20 are less inclined to the physical, even they are not totally removed from it. See D. J. A. Clines, "The Etymology of Hebrew *SELEM*," *Journal of Northwest Semitic Languages* 3 (1974): 19–25, and his "The Image

of God in Man," *Tyndale Bulletin* 19 (1968): 53–103; J. M. Miller, "In the 'Image' and 'Likeness' of God," *Journal of Biblical Literature* 91 (1972): 289–304. On the surface, the use of "likeness" (*dĕmût*) is a bit less physical, but even this word can be used of visions or images that correspond to physical objects (Ezek. 1:22; 10:21; 23:15; and esp. 2 Kings 16:10 and 2 Chron. 4:3). Also see J. Piper, "The Image of God: An Approach from Biblical and Systematic Theology," *Studia Biblica et Theologica* 1 (1971): 15–32.

11. Manahan, "Reexamination," 219.

12. Genesis 1:28.

13. In fact, the Bible later presents heaven as a thriving community of people who live in peace and wholeness. On the other hand, it depicts hell as a foreboding place with a notable absence of the qualities of heaven.

14. Though *rādâ*, "rule," may have the idea of force added to it, the word can be used to describe appropriate *supervisory* work initiated by the central government (1 Kings 5:16 [MT 5:30]; 9:23; 2 Chron. 8:10); see J. Limburg, "What Does It Mean to have Dominion over the Earth?" *Dialogue* 10 (1972): 221–23. *Kābaš*, "subdue," is a more aggressive term. Its use in Esther 7:8 shows the violence with which it can be associated. Beyond this, it is used for the subjugation of foreign peoples (Num. 32:22, 29; Josh. 18:1; 2 Sam. 8:11; 1 Chron. 22:18), of sins being trodden underfoot (Mic. 7:19), and bringing others to slavery (Jer. 34:11, 16; Neh. 5:5 [twice]; 2 Chron. 28:10.)

15. George W. Coats concluded that the principal concern of ruling and subduing is productivity: "The focus falls on fruitful productivity, not destructive over-production or exploitation; on use of power for particular ends, not unlimited power, on life, not death" ("The God of Death," *Journal of Bible and Theology* 29 [1975]: 229). Walter J. Dumbrell summed up the role human beings in creation: ". . . man is installed as God's vice-gerent over all creation with power to control and regulate it, to harness its clear potential. . . ." ("Genesis 1–3, Ecology, and the Dominion of Man," *Crux* 21 [1985]: 19).

16. An especially helpful and extensive treatment of the subject can be found in H.

K. Havice, "The Concern for the Widow and the Fatherless in the Ancient Near East: A Case Study in Old Testament Ethics" (Ph.D. diss., Yale University, 1978).

17. See B. F. Lowe, "The King As Mediator of the Cosmic Order" (Ph.D. diss., Emory University, 1967).

18. See 2 Samuel 21:1–6; Psalm 72; Isaiah 32.

19. For example, Psalm 72 projects a time when an ideal king will obey God; prosperity (Heb. *šālôm*, vv. 3, 7), justice (*mišpāṭ*, vv. 1, 2), and righteousness (*šedeq*, v. 2) are the words used to describe the kingdom then.

20. D. N. Steele and C. C. Thomas, *Romans: An Interpretive Outline* (Philadelphia: Presbyterian and Reformed, 1963), 44.

21. Romans 5:17.

22. Hebrewt *šedeq*, "righteousness," is broad in its meaning, a breadth shown also in Ugaritic. Both J. Swetman ("Some Observations on the Background of *Tsedeq* in Jeremias 23,5a," *Biblica* 46 [1965]: 29–40) and C. H. Gordon (*Ugaritic Textbook* [*Analecta Orientalia*, 38; Rome: Pontificum Institutum Biblicum, 1965], 472–73, no. 2147) described this Ugaritic usage. "In the case of Psalm 72:3 the meaning of *tsedeq* appears to be that a kingship properly endowed by God will result in that productivity which God has destined for his people" (Manahan, "Reexamination," 175).

23. See Leonhard Goppelt, *Typos: The Typological Interpretation of the Old Testament in the New*, trans. Donald H. Madvig (Grand Rapids: Eerdmans, 1982). Goppelt called attention to the importance of historical correspondence and escalation in typological interpretation.

24. 1 Corinthians 15:20–28.

25. Ephesians 1:19–23; Colossians 1:15–20.

26. On this, Hebrews 2:5–9 is a most important passage. Essentially, through use of the Genesis 1 and Psalm 8 materials, it presents Christ as *the* solution to all relationships.

27. As quoted in D. E. Shoemaker, "Loving People, Loving Earth," *Christianity and Crisis* 47 (1987): 261.

Chapter 3

1. For a critical interpretation, see Susan P. Bratton, "Ecotheology of James Watt," *Environmental Ethics* 5 (1983): 225–36.

2. 2 Timothy 3:16–17.

3. Jaroslav Pelikan, *The Christian Tradition: A History of the Development of Doctrine I: The Emergence of the Catholic Tradition (100-600)* (Chicago: University of Chicago, 1971), 75.

4. Ibid., 73.

5. Ibid.

6. 2 Peter 3:13.

7. The image is derived from the practice of torturing witches to extract confessions from them.

8. On this point, see O. H. Steck, *World and Environment* (Nashville: Abingdon, 1980), 229–31, 258–61. Herman Bavinck, in his 1894 essay on "Common Grace" (translated by Raymond C. Van Leeuwen, *Calvin Theological Journal* 24 [1989]: 35–65]), made a similar point about the different focus of the Old and New Testaments: "So perfectly is grace the content of New Testament religion that the attributes of God seen in nature and the creation become less prominent [than in the Old Testament]. They are not, however, denied but are rather everywhere presupposed, while in the foreground we find emphasized God's attributes of love, grace, and peace. . . . God's relation to nature retreats to give pride of place to the relationship between God and his church" (p. 43).

9. For basic treatments of Paul's thought, including Old Testament roots and creational presuppositions, see esp. Herman Ridderbos, *Paul: An Outline of his Theology* (Grand Rapids: Eerdmans, 1975), and Seyoon Kim, *The Origin of Paul's Gospel* (Grand Rapids: Eerdmans, 1982).

10. 1 Corinthians 1:18–2:2.

11 There is a long and influential history of interpretation that reads the Gospel of John as an "otherworldly," quasi-Gnostic book. (See H. Paul Santmire's otherwise valuable book, *The Travail of Nature: the Ambiguous Ecological Promise of Christian Theology* [Philadelphia: Fortress, 1985], 211–13.) In this century Rudolph Bultmann is a key example. But it is precisely John's repeated emphasis on the resurrection (e.g., "I will raise him up" in John 6:40, 44, 54; cf. 2:19, 20; 6:39) and on the cosmic Christ of John 1 that forbids such a reading. For Bultmann and Santmire such emphases on creation and resurrection are merely the inconsistent work of later editors. I am indebted to my colleague David Holwerda for discussion on this point.

12. Oliver O'Donovan, *Resurrection and Moral Order: An Outline for Evangelical Ethics* (Leicester, England: Inter-Varsity; Grand Rapids: Eerdmans, 1986), 13–14.

13. On this passage as a whole, see Ridderbos, *Paul*, 78–86. Detailed treatments may be found in the commentaries of Ridderbos, *Aan de Kolossenzen* (Kampen: Kok, 1960), and Eduard Lohse, *Colossians and Philemon* (Philadelphia: Fortress, 1971), 41–61.

14. On the cosmic scope and character of redemption, see Ridderbos, *Paul*, 89, 159.

15. In a monumental study, W. D. Davies states that "Paul ignores completely the territorial aspect of the [Abrahamic] promise. The land is not within his purview" (*The Gospel and the Land: Early Christianity and Jewish Territorial Doctrine* [Berkeley: University of California, 1974], 178; also see 18). This is most curious in the light of Romans 4:13, which Davies cited but never explicitly discussed. Paul's extraordinary statement that Abraham and his descendents by faith would inherit "the world" is nowhere literally found in the Old Testament. But Paul is clearly working out the implications of the Abrahamic promises and is playing on the ambiguity of Hebrew 'ereš, which means both "land" and "earth/world."

Walter Brueggeman (*The Land: Place as Gift, Promise, and Challenge in Biblical Faith* [Philadelphia: Fortress, 1977], 177) notes that, based on mere frequency of word usage, Davies might appear right about Paul's lack of interest in the land. But Brueggemann rightly points out that Paul's use of Abraham as his model for faith in Romans 4 and Galatians 3–4 shows Paul's concern for the land. In fact Paul's language shows that God's redemptive promise of an inheritance includes not just the land of Israel but the entire world (Rom. 4:13; also see 8:17, 19–25; Gal. 3:14, 18; 4:7, 28).

16. Romans 4:24–25. For the grammar of Gk. *dia* ("for"), see the commentaries of Ridderbos, *Aan de Romeinen* (Kampen: Kok, 1959), and Ernst Käsemann, *Commentary on Romans* (Grand Rapids: Eerdmans, 1980), 128–29. In Paul the Greek word translated "justification" is a sibling of the word "righteousness" (they both belong to the *dikē* word-group). On Romans 4:25 as a whole, see Ulrich Wilckens, *Der Brief an die Römer*, I (Zürich: Benzinger Verlag; Neukirchen: Neukirchener Verlag, 1978), 278–80.

17. For example, Romans 5:9; see 1 Timothy 3:16.

18. Romans 5:1.

19. See Philippians 3:10, 21.

20. Colossians 3:10; 1 Corinthians 15. The theme of first and second Adam cannot and need not be developed here in the light of Ronald Manahan's essay in this volume, "Christ as Second Adam," 45–56.

21. For a rich treatment of this Pauline theme, see Kim, *The Origin of Paul's Gospel*, 137–268.

22. Ephesians 4:24.

23. Romans 6:4.

24. Romans 6:13.

25. Romans 8:11.

26. Romans 8:10.

27. Romans 8:18–30. It is beyond the scope of this essay to treat the important creation text in Romans 8:18–30. Against attempts to restrict the word "creation" (*ktisis*) in this passage to the merely human, see Käsemann, *Commentary on Romans*, 229–45. See also Walther Bindemann, *Die Hoffnung der Schöpfung: Römer 8,18–27 und die Frage einer Theologie der Befreiung von Mensch und Natur* (Neukirchen-Vluyn: Neukirchener Verlag, 1983).

28. Romans 8:2, 4.

29. H. H. Schmid is perhaps the key scholar in this movement. While aspects of his work have been criticized, I consider its basic thrust unassailable. H. H. Schmid, "Creation, Righteousness, and Salvation: 'Creation Theology' as the Broad Horizon of Biblical Theology," in *Creation in the Old Testament*, ed. Bernard W. Anderson (Philadelphia: Fortress, 1984), 102–17. Unfortunately, this English translation of Schmid's article lacks the section treating the New Testament. That article can be found in Schmid's collection of essays, *Altorientalische Welt in der alttestamentlichen Theologie* (Zürich: Theologischer Verlag, 1974). Also, see Schmid's *Gerechtigkeit als Weltordnung* (Tübingen: J. C. B. Mohr [Paul Siebeck], 1968), and his "Rechtfertigung als Schöpfungsgeschehen: Notizen zur alttestamentlichen Vorgeschichte eines neutestamentlichen Themas," in *Rechtfertigung. Festschrift für Ernst Käsemann*, ed. J. Friedrich, W. Pöhlman, and Peter Stuhlmacher (Göttingen: Vandenhoeck und Ruprecht, 1976), 403–14. For further scholarly treatment, see Rolf Knierim, "Cosmos and History in Israel's Theology," *Horizons in Biblical Theology* 3 (1981): 59–123; "The Task of Old Testament Theology," *Horizons in Biblical Theology* 6 (1984): 25–57; U. Luck, "Gerechtigkeit in der Welt—Gerechtigkeit Gottes," *Wort und Dienst* 12 (1973): 71–89; Peter Stuhlmacher, "Erwägungen zum ontologischen Charakter der [*kainē ktisis*] bei Paulus," *Evangelische Theologie* 27 (1967): 1–35; and Ernst Käsemann, "The 'Righteousness of God' in Paul," in *New Testament Questions for Today* (Philadelphia: Fortress, 1969), 168–82. I judge that H. Ridderbos still took justification in too narrow a sense (*Paul*, 160–64), even though elsewhere he clearly saw the cosmic scope of redemption. Justification is always a cosmic act.

30. See Kim, *The Origin of Paul's Gospel*, 313–29, for the close connection between justification, reconciliation, and new creation.

31. Stuhlmacher, "Erwägungen," 2 (author's translation).

32. Some have read the "dominion" and "subdue it" of Genesis 1:26–28 (cf. Ps. 8), as warranting exploitation and degradation of the earth. But this is in conflict with the Old Testament understanding of earthly kingship. Earthly kings (in this case Adam or "humankind") are vassal-stewards of the divine king. Their responsibility before God is to rule for the well-being (*šālôm*) of their subjects, including the natural realm. Moreover, the king's wisdom and justice are conducive to the fertility of the earth (Ps. 72). Kings rule in accordance with *cosmic* Wisdom (Prov. 8:15–16). Psalm 65 portrays the divine King's beneficent rule over his people and the fruitfulness of the earth which

attends it. See further, K. W. Whitelam, *The Just King: Monarchical and Judicial Authority in Ancient Israel* (Sheffield: JSOT Press, 1979); Schmid, *Gerechtigkeit*; and Gerhard von Rad, *Wisdom In Israel* (Nashville: Abingdon, 1972), chap. 9.

33. The key passage in Paul is 1 Corinthians 7:29–31, which concludes, "For this world in its present form is passing away" (NIV). On this passage, see Gordon D. Fee, *The First Epistle to the Corinthians* (Grand Rapids: Eerdmans, 1987), 334–42.

34. See A. Wolters, "Worldview and Textual Criticism in 2 Peter 3:10," *Westminster Theological Journal* 49 (1987): 407–13. The text of the passage and its metallurgical imagery actually mean that the world will be refined by fire and appear (*heurethesetai*) purified.

35. Or "psychical" (Gk. *psychikos*). Paul's reference is to Genesis 2:7 as 1 Corinthians 15:45 makes clear.

36. Christoph Burchard, "1 Korinther 15:39–41," *Zeitschrift für die neutestamentliche Wissenschaft* 75 (1984), 237–39.

37. True, human bodies are "sown in dishonor" and "raised in honor" (v. 43). Yet this is not a commentary on the evil of present bodies per se. Rather, it means first that our present bodily life has not reached the ultimate goal of its creation, to attain a body like the glorified body of Christ, the "image of God" made perfect. Second, it means that our present existence and glory has been radically marred by sin (Rom. 3:23).

38. 1 Timothy 6:13, 16.

39. See O'Donovan, *Resurrection and Moral Order*, 31–52, for the crucial role of generic "kinds" for a Christian worldview and ethics.

40. 1 Corinthians 15:35–36.

41. See Matthew 6:1–4. The translation of *dikaiosunē* as "piety" in the RSV is unfortunate. The word literally is "righteousness." Compare the NIV translation of Matthew 6:1 and the comment in the *NIV Study Bible*: "This verse introduces the discussion of three acts of righteousness: (1) giving (vv. 2–4), (2) praying (vv. 5–15) and (3) fasting (vv. 16–18)." Note that each section including vv. 5–15 ends with a discussion of *reward*. Fasting is profoundly con-

nected to our use and stewardship of earthly goods, as well as to our neighbor's poverty.

42. 2 Corinthians 5:10. This passage has implications for our work in the world far beyond the confines of the "church" and evangelism, narrowly conceived (see Rom. 2:6–11; 1 Cor. 3:10–15). Incidentally, none of these passages compromise the doctrine of justification by grace alone, though they do stand in apparently paradoxical relation to it.

43. Steck, *World and Environment*, 266.

44. 2 Corinthians 5:14–15.

45. Galatians 3:27; see also Romans 13:14; Colossians 3:10, 12.

46. 2 Corinthians 5:17–18. On the meaning and translation of this passage, see Victor P. Furnish, *II Corinthians* (Garden City, N.Y.: Doubleday, 1984), 314–20. In verse 17 the Greek is literally, "So that if anyone is in Christ, a new creation. . . ." In verse 18 Gk. *ta panta* (lit. "all things"; NIV "all this") is a common expression that regularly refers to creation as a whole. For a close parallel, see Romans 11:36: "For from him and through him and to him are *all things*" [italics added].

47. Steck, *World and Environment*, 249; Stuhlmacher, "Erwägungen," 1–35.

48. In this translation the italicized words *old things* (Gk. *ta archaia*), *Behold* (Gk. *idou*), and *new things* (Gk. *kaina*) all appear in 2 Corinthians 5:17; however, the NIV does not translate Gk. *idou* ("behold") in 2 Corinthians 5:17 but instead uses an exclamation point to catch the nuance. The translation of the Septuagint here has been modified from Sir Lancelot C. L. Brenton, *The Septuagint with Apocrypha: Greek and English* (Grand Rapids: Zondervan, n.d.). See also Isaiah 42:9; 48:6–7.

49. See 2 Peter 3:13; Revelation 21:1–5.

50. Steck, *World and Environment*, 289–90, 293.

51. Romans 6:4–13; 8:4; 2 Corinthians 5:21.

52. Romans 13:8–10.

53. See Raymond C. Van Leeuwen, "Enjoying Creation—Within Limits," *Christianity Today*, 12 May 1989.

54. See Paul's strong statements on greed: "the greedy . . . will [not] inherit the kingdom of God" (1 Cor. 6:10; see 5:11). For the converse positive implications, see

Harvie M. Conn, "Christ and the City: Biblical Themes for Building Urban Theology Models," in *Discipling the City: Theological Reflections on Urban Mission*, ed. Roger S. Greenway (Grand Rapids: Baker, 1979), 258.

55. Romans 13:13–14.

56. Romans 14:17, 20–21, 23.

57. For the connection of the dietary laws to creation theology and their rich implications for a theology of holiness, see the introductory section to Gordon Wenham's *The Book of Leviticus* (Grand Rapids: Eerdmans, 1979).

58. Colossians 3:17.

59. 2 Corinthians 5:17–18; Galatians 6:15.

60. Matthew 6:26, 28–29; 1 Corinthians 15:40–41.

61. Romans 11:36.

Chapter 4

1. For helpful comments on biblical interpretation in respect to the present topic, see Loren Wilkinson, "New Age, New Consciousness, and the New Creation," in *Tending the Garden: Essays on the Gospel and the Earth*, ed. Wesley Granberg-Michaelson (Grand Rapids: Eerdmans, 1987), 27–29. On "ecological hermeneutics," particularly in the face of the ambiguous or seemingly contradictory witness to this topic in the New Testament, see H. Paul Santmire, *The Travail of Nature: The Ambiguous Ecological Promise of Christian Theology* (Philadelphia: Fortress, 1985); Douglas J. Hall, *Imaging God: Dominion as Stewardship* (Grand Rapids: Eerdmans, 1986).

2. See J. Christian Beker, *Paul the Apostle: The Triumph of God in Life and Thought* (Philadelphia: Fortress, 1980). For the thesis that Paul's apocalyptic theology is rich in ecologically significant ideas, see Santmire, *Travail of Nature*, 208.

3. Although "kingdom" is not in the original French title, kingdom themes are prominent in Jacques Ellul's *The Presence of the Kingdom* (New York: Seabury, 1967). See also John Howard Yoder, *The Politics of Jesus* (Grand Rapids: Eerdmans, 1972);

idem, *The Priestly Kingdom* (South Bend: University of Notre Dame, 1984); D. Kraybill, *The Upside-Down Kingdom* (Scottdale, Pa.: Herald, 1978); and Stanley Hauerwas, *The Peaceable Kingdom* (South Bend: University of Notre Dame, 1983).

4. These last two questions are two of the three key questions in Granberg-Michaelson, *Tending the Garden*, 3–4.

5. For example, John Macquarrie, "Creation and Environment," *Expository Times* 83 (1971): 4–9; Gordon Kaufmann, *Theology for a Nuclear Age* (Philadelphia: Westminster, 1985); Sally McFague, *Models of God: Theology for an Ecological, Nuclear Age* (Philadelphia: Fortress, 1987). Space does not permit an adequate discussion of this challenge.

6. George E. Ladd, *The Presence of the Future* (Grand Rapids: Eerdmans, 1974), 45.

7. See, e.g., Ernst Käsemann, "On the Subject of Primitive Christian Apocalyptic," in *New Testament Questions of Today* (Philadelphia: Fortress, 1969), 108–37.

8. See, e.g., John Bright, *The Kingdom of God* (Nashville: Abingdon, 1953).

9. For example, Psalms 103:19; 145:13.

10. For example, Psalms 74:12–17; 89:9–13; 93:1–4; 95:3–5; 96:5, 10; 97:6; 104:7–9; Job 38:8–11; Isaiah 51:9. See B. Ollenburger, *Zion, the City of the Great King* (Sheffield: JSOT Press, 1987).

11. For example, 2 Kings 19:15; Psalms 29:10; 47:2; 93; 96:10; 97; 99:1–4; 145:11ff.; Isaiah 6:5; Jeremiah 46:18.

12. For example, Psalm 24:4–6.

13. Genesis 3.

14. For example, Psalms 18:7–15; 93:1–4.

15. For example, Isaiah 11:1–9.

16. Isaiah 32:15–18; 35:1–2, 10; 41:19; 51:3; 55:13; 60:13; 65:17–25.

17. Ladd, *The Presence of the Future*, 60–62.

18. See, e.g., Zechariah 14:9: "The Lord will be king over the whole earth. On that day there will be one LORD, and his name the only name."

19. For example, Isaiah 13:13; 51:6; Amos 8:8–9; Joel 3:30–31; Haggai 2:6–7.

20. Seeds of this development are already evident in Joel, Isaiah 24–27, and Zechariah 9–14. The literature on Jewish apocalyptic thought and literature is becom-

ing voluminous. See, e.g., Klaus Koch, *The Rediscovery of Apocalyptic* (London: SCM, 1972); and John J. Collins, *The Apocalyptic Imagination* (New York: Crossroad, 1984).

21. This threefold summary is based on Beker, *Paul the Apostle*, 135–37.

22. See, e.g., G. R. Beasley-Murray, *Revelation* (Grand Rapids: Eerdmans, 1978), 306–7. For replacement, see, e.g., 1 Enoch 72:1; 83:3–9; 91:14ff. For transformation, see, e.g., 1 Enoch 45:4–5; 2 Baruch 3:4ff.; 32:6; 57:2; 4 Ezra 7:29ff.

23. For example, 1 Enoch 91–105.

24. Space does not permit a consideration of the variations within Jewish apocalyptic thought, including (1) the end can come with or without a mediator; (2) salvation can mean especially national deliverance or a universal judgment; (3) sometimes there is an intermediate messianic kingdom in the age prior to the age to come; and (4) responses ranging from martyrdom to warfare are held up as the proper role of the people of God in bringing the kingdom.

25. For a presentation that includes these four aspects, see O. E. Evans, "Kingdom of God, of Heaven," in *Interpreter's Dictionary of the Bible*, ed. George A. Buttrick (Nashville: Abingdon, 1962), 3:17–26. See also George E. Ladd, "Kingdom of God," in *International Standard Bible Encyclopedia*, ed. Geoffrey W. Bromiley (Grand Rapids: Eerdmans, 1986), 3:23–29. The secondary literature on the kingdom of God in the New Testament is very extensive. For a useful sampling, see Richard H. Hiers, "Kingdom of God," in *Interpreter's Dictionary of the Bible: Supplementary Volume*, ed. Keith Crim (Nashville: Abingdon, 1976), 516.

26. Revelation 4:10–11.

27. Acts 4:24; 14:15; 17:24; Romans 1:20–25; 4:17; 1 Corinthians 10:26; 11:19 (cf. Mark 10:6); Ephesians 3:9; 1 Timothy 4:3; Revelation 10:6; for incidental references, see Matthew 25:34; Mark 13:19 (Matt. 24:21); 13:35 (Luke 11:15); 1 Peter 1:20; Revelation 13:8; 17:8.

28. For texts connecting God's lordship and creation, see Acts 4:24; 17:24; Revelation 4. For the theme of the cosmic role of Christ as creator, see John 1:2, 10; 17:24; Colossians 1:15–20; Hebrews 1:1–3, 10; 2:10; Revelation 3:14. For a discussion of the implications of this theme for Christian environmental stewardship, see Loren Wilkinson's essay in this volume, "Christ as Creator and Redeemer," 25–44.

29. For example, Matthew 5:19, 20; 7:21; 8:11 (Luke 13:28); 18:3; Mark 9:47; 10:15 (Luke 18:17); 10:23–25 (Matt. 19:21; Luke 18:24); 14:25 (Matt. 18:24); 1 Corinthians 6:9–10; Galatians 5:21; Ephesians 5:5; 1 Thessalonians 2:12; 2 Timothy 4:1, 18; Hebrews 12:28; James 2:5; Revelation 11:25; 12:10; 22:5.

30. See also Romans 11:36; Revelation 21:22–22:5.

31. For a discussion of the ecological implications of the comprehensive redoing—personal, social, and cosmic—by Christ the second Adam in the face of the undoing of creation by the first Adam, see Ronald Manahan's essay in this volume, "Christ as the Second Adam," 45–56.

32. Romans 8:23.

33. 1 Corinthians 15:26.

34. Note the connection of God's reign and resurrection in 1 Corinthians 15. Resurrection and life in Paul also have cosmic implications beyond the merely personal; see R. Van Leeuwen's essay in this volume, "Christ's Resurrection and the Creation's Vindication," 57–71.

35. For example, Psalms 72; 85:10; 97:2; Isaiah 32:17.

36. See Perry Yoder, *Shalom: The Bible's Word for Salvation, Justice, and Peace* (Newton, Kans.: Faith and Life Press, 1987).

37. Matthew 22:1–10; Mark 14:25; Luke 13:29; 14:15; 22:30; Revelation 19:6–9.

38. Romans 8:31–39; Revelation 21:22–22:5.

39. Revelation 11:15–18.

40. Revelation 11:18; 19:2.

41. Revelation 21:1.

42. Revelation 21:5.

43. W. Bauer, *A Greek-English Lexicon of the New Testament and Other Early Christian Literature*, trans. and adapted by W. F. Arndt and F. W. Gingrich, 2d ed. rev. and augmented by F. W. Gingrich and F. W. Danker, (Chicago: University of Chicago Press, 1979), s.v. ἀποκατάστασις.

44. This is true if one takes the conjunction "and" (Gk. καί) in 1 Thessalonians 2:12 as an ascensive.

45. See Paulos M. Gregorios, "New Testament Foundations for Understanding Creation," in *Tending the Garden: Essays on the Gospel and the Earth*, ed. Wesley Granberg-Michaelson (Grand Rapids: Eerdmans, 1987), 84–87.

46. 2 Corinthians 5:17; Galatians 6:15.

47. 2 Corinthians 5:19; see also Colossians 1:20.

48. Colossians 3:10; see also Romans 8:29; 1 Corinthians 15:29; 2 Corinthians 3:18; Ephesians 4:24.

49. See, e.g., Victor P. Furnish, *II Corinthians* (Garden City, N.Y.: Doubleday, 1984), 314–19, 332–36.

50. See 1 Corinthians 15:25–28; Ephesians 1:10, 22 ("all things"); Philippians 3:21; Colossians 1:20 ("all things"); see also Romans 8:28–39; 11:36; Hebrews 1:2; 2:8–9. Similarly, the Gospel of John speaks of Christ as both Creator (1:3, 10) and Savior of the *kosmos* (3:16–17; 4:42; 12:47). While the latter texts are articulated in terms of human redemption (e.g., 3:16–21), the meaning of these references seems to include the entirety of creation. See Loren Wilkinson's essay in this volume, "Christ as Creator and Redeemer," 25–44.

51. Romans 4:13.

52. Matthew 5:5.

53. See Matthew 5:3, 10.

54. Revelation 5:10.

55. Revelation 20:1–6.

56. Revelation 22:1–5; See Beasley-Murray, *Revelation*, 127–28; George E. Ladd, *Revelation* (Grand Rapids: Eerdmans, 1972), 91–93. Revelation 1:6 also refers to the present kingship of Christians.

57. Matthew 6:10.

58. See Ladd, *Presence of the Future.*

59. Matthew 12:28; Luke 11:20.

60. Mark 10:15.

61. Luke 17:21.

62. Matthew 6:33; Luke 12:31.

63. Matthew 6:10.

64. Donald Kraybill, *The Upside-Down Kingdom* (Scottdale, Pa.: Herald, 1978).

65. Matthew 19:14; 21:31; 23:13; 25:34ff.

66. Matthew 18:1–4; 19:23–24; 20:1–6; Luke 1:46–55.

67. Matthew 20:20–28.

68. Jesus' healing is described as "saving a *psychē*" (Mark 3:4), which illustrates the Hebrew concept of a person as an animated body, not an embodied, imprisoned soul, as in Platonic thought. Care for the body was an integral part of Jesus' spiritual mission. The importance of creation in the teachings of Jesus is also evident in (1) his use of wisdom instruction based on the observation of the created world (e.g., Matt. 5:45), (2) the many parables of stewardship, and (3) direct arguments on the basis of creation (Mark 10:6).

69. See esp. Beker, *Paul the Apostle*, 135–81. See also R. Van Leeuwen's essay in this volume, "Christ's Resurrection and the Creation's Vindication," 57–71.

70. Colossians 1:12–13.

71. Romans 14:17.

72. Colossians 2:9–15.

73. It should also be observed that the concept of "being in Christ" is social, not merely individual (esp. Gal. 3:26–29); moreover, since the goal of redemption is the reconciliation of all things in Christ, the concept also has a cosmic scope.

74. Colossians 4:11.

75. 2 Corinthians 5:17–21.

76. Francis Schaeffer, *Pollution and the Death of Man: The Christian View of Ecology* (Wheaton, Ill.: Tyndale, 1970), 68–69.

77. Thus, Paul can stress either aspect. For Corinth, where believers are stressing the present spiritual reality of the resurrection and denying its future horizon, Paul emphasizes the still-to-come aspect of salvation. For Colossae, where believers think they are presently under the control of cosmic powers that must be appeased through asceticism, Paul stresses that Christ has already gained victory.

78. Matthew 5:20; 7:21.

79. See Ellul, *Presence of the Kingdom*, 61–95.

80. Matthew 5:9.

81. John 18:36.

82. For example, C. Redekop, "Toward a Mennonite Theology and Ethic of Creation," *Mennonite Quarterly Review* 60 (1986): 387–403; J. Carmody, *Ecology and Religion: Toward a New Christian Theology of Nature* (New York: Paulist, 1983).

83. Isaiah 11:9; 65:25.

84. Revelation 11:18; 19:2.

85. The vision of Revelation 17:1–19:4 closely connects greed and the earth's

destruction: the insatiable desire for consumption and wealth is what results in the destruction of people and the earth. While this text describes the 1st-century Roman world, it is also a powerful metaphor of the present world and its subjugation at the hands of multinational corporations.

86. For example, Loren Wilkinson, ed., *Earthkeeping: Christian Stewardship of Natural Resources* (Grand Rapids: Eerdmans, 1980), 72–94, 239–49; Wesley Ganberg-Michaelson, *A Wordly Spirituality* (San Francisco: Harper & Row, 1984), 85–90; McFague, *Models of God*, 52 n.34.

87. Matthew 5:14–16.

88. Ibid. For the meaning of Gk. *halas* as "fertilizer" in this context, see esp. Luke 14:34–35.

89. Mark 13:31 (Matt. 24:35; Luke 21:33); Matthew 5:18 (Luke 16:17); Hebrews 1:10–12 (cf. 12:26–29); 1 John 2:17; 2 Peter 3:5–13; Revelation 21:1, 4; cf. 2 Corinthians 5:17; 1 Corinthians 7:31.

90. Hebrews 1:10–12; 12:26–29; 2 Peter 3:5–13; Revelation 21:1 (cf. 6:12ff.; 8:6–12; 16:1–11; 20:11). For the motif of cosmic cataclysm in the Old Testament, see note 19 above.

91. Romans 8:17–23; 2 Corinthians 5:17.

92. 1 Corinthians 7:31.

93. See 2 Peter 3:5–13, which uses the metaphor of metallurgical refinement. Hebrews 12:26–29 uses the metaphor of cosmic shaking to show the separation of good and evil in creation.

94. Revelation 11:18; 19:2.

95. Ladd, *Revelation*, 275.

96. The notion that the degradation of earth is God-ordained and a sign of the times announcing the imminent arrival of Christ's return is perhaps the most dangerous response voiced by Christians, leading to a complete social and ecological irresponsibility. The Book of Revelation does not predict present-day pollution, and to read Revelation as a key to time-tabling the future is to miss the primary message of the book. On this problem, see Granberg-Michaelson, *A Worldly Spirituality*, 105–17.

97. Certain New Testament texts emphasize the earthly-heavenly dualism, e.g., Colossians 2:20; 3:2; 2 Corinthians 4:16–5:5; 5:8. In the Colossian passages, however, the reference is to an ethical dualism and does not imply a negative evaluation of earth as such. Cf. John 18:36; James 3:13–18. And while the Corinthian passages refer to the hope that death in Christ means immediate fellowship with the Lord (cf. Phil. 2), Paul never relaxes the future-oriented dimension of ultimate salvation. See also Beker (*Paul the Apostle*, 160–63) on ways in which the apocalyptic framework is transposed to either postponement (Luke-Acts; 2 Peter) or spiritualization (John; Hebrews) in some of the later New Testament writings. It should be observed, however, that in the Eastern Orthodox tradition, realized eschatology is the basis for a sacramental view of the cosmos, not a world-denying spiritualizing. For the promise of the Eastern Orthodox perspective for Christian environmental stewardship, see Wilkinson, *Earthkeeping*.

Chapter 5

1. Luke 24:7.

2. The assertion that the Christianity of my youth was of little practical effect in the building up of society is off the mark in one respect: The churches in which I grew up all did, and still do, excellent work in terms of dealing with drug and alcohol abuse, distressed or broken marriages, and disturbed children. In this way they have made a genuine contribution to society. Our church members did not lie or steal, paid their taxes, were honest on the job, practiced marital fidelity, and helped the poor. These practices, however, were largely matters of private morality. Consequently, the care and concern that we applied to ourselves and those close to us did not extend in any great degree to the polity, economy, and society in which we participated, or to the natural world.

3. The attempt to plumb the meaning of the life of Jesus for ecological ethics has apologetic implications. If the church cannot show *how* Jesus is Lord of the ecological crisis, then it will have a problem not only in ecological ethics but in apologetics as well.

4. Matthew 6:28–29.

5. Matthew 10:29–31; Luke 12:6–8.

6. As one of the primary contemporary defenders of the Christian standpoint in ecological ethics, Wendel Berry says that Christians need to become more earthy. Obviously, his suggestion does not apply to Jesus himself, who never had to deal with the suspicion about the nonspiritual order inherited from the Greek philosophical heritage.

7. See, e.g., Deuteronomy 11:13–17.

8. David Ehrenfeld, "Judaism and the Practice of Stewardship," *Judaism* 34 (1985): 304.

9. Ibid., 307.

10. The practice of the Sabbath and of the Sabbath year were fairly prominent features in the life of certain parts of the Jewish community. That the Jubilee was ever practiced, however, is in dispute. The existence of the institution of the *prosboul*, by which a person could sign over his debts to a third party so that they could be collected in spite of the ban on their direct collection, would seem to indicate indirectly that in some sectors the Jubilee *was* practiced (there would be no need for the *prosboul* if the practice of remitting debts every fifty years were not practiced). The *prosboul* was invented by the Pharisee Hillel, the grandfather of Gamaliel, the teacher of Paul. See John H. Yoder, *The Politics of Jesus* (Grand Rapids: Eerdmans, 1972), 69.

11. Psalm 93:5.

12. For the most part, a separation between religion and politics was literally unthinkable before the advent of the modern secular state, which in turn was a creative response to the religious wars of the post-Reformation period. Because we assume that a separation between religion and politics is possible, we assume that it was possible in Jesus' time.

13. For some reason, this aspect of Jesus' ministry has been clear to many outside the community of New Testament Christians. Both Gandhi and Martin Luther King, Jr., besides being attracted to the moral and religious character of Jesus, were also attracted to his ability to build power out of a situation of powerlessness, sickness, and oppression. Jay Haley is the most recent secular observer of this phenomenon (see his *The Power Tactics of Jesus Christ* [New York: Avon Books, 1969]); John H. Yoder is the most perceptive evangelical student of this (see his *The Politics of Jesus* [Grand Rapids: Eerdmans, 1972]).

Epilogue

1. Wendell Barry, *Home Economics* (San Francisco: North Point Press, 1987), 44.

Appendix

1. Mary Anglemyer, Eleanor R. Seagraves, and Catherine C. LeMaistre, *A Search for Environmental Ethics: An Initial Bibliography* (Washington, D. C.: Smithsonian Instituition Press, 1980). Fred G. Van Dyke, *An Introductory Bibliography on Planetheonomics with Selected Annotations* (an unpublished paper presented at the 1986 Au Sable Forum, Mancelona, Mich., 1986).

2. Henry B. D. Suld, "The Relation of the Doctrine of Creation to the Person of Jesus Christ in New Testament Theology" (Ph.D. diss., McGill University, 1961), H. J. Hammerton, "Unity of Creation in the Apocalypse," *Church Quarterly Review* 168 (1967): 20–33, H. Paul Santmire, *Brother Earth: Nature, God, and Ecology in a Time of Crisis* (New York: Thomas Nelson, 1970), John G. Gibbs, *Creation and Redemption: A Study in Pauline Theology* (Leiden: Brill, 1971), Joseph Sittler, *Essays on Nature and Grace* (Philadelphia: Fortress, 1972), and H. Paul Santmire, *The Travail of Nature: The Ambiguous Ecological Promise of Christian Theology* (Philadelphia: Fortress, 1985).

3. Santmire, *Travail of Nature*, 217–18.

4. Louis H. Taylor, *The New Creation: A Study of the Pauline Doctrine of Creation, Innocence, Sin, and Redemption* (New York: Pagent, 1958).

5. Gordon Kaufman, "The Concept of Nature: A Problem for Theology," *Harvard Theological Review* 65 (1972): 350.

6. Only sources directly discussing the biblical theology of creation were sought.

7. Stacey (1956), Taylor (1958), Bring (1964), Ditmanson (1964), Wood (1964), Engel (1970), Shepherd (1970), Sittler (1970), Gibbs (1971), Granberg-Michaelson (1971), Williams (1971), Calhoun (1972), Maahs (1972), Reumann (1973), McDonald (1974), Scott (1974), Welbourne (1975), Dalton (1977), Landes (1978), Yoder (1978), Lincoln (1981), McIntyre (1981), Stewart (1983), Anderson (in Joransen and Butigan, 1984), Hiers (1984), Joransen and Butigan (1984), Gregorios (in Granberg-Michaelson, 1987). A number of these references are given in full in other notes. Those which are not may be found in "A Working-Draft Bibliography on Christian Stewardship of Creation," available from Au Sable Institute, Mancelona, Michigan.

8. George H. Williams, "Christian Attitudes Towards Nature Parts 1, 2," *Christian Scholars Review* 2 (1971): 3–35, 112–26.

9. Hugh Montefiore, "Ecology, Theology and Posterity," *New Scientist and Science Journal* 49 (1971): 316–18.

10. In Philip N. Joransen and Ken Butigan, eds., *Cry of the Environment: Rebuilding the Christian Creation Tradition* (Sante Fe: Bear and Company, 1984).

11. Ibid.

12. Ibid.

13. Maahs, "The Theology of Human Ecological Responsibility in the Old Testament."

14. Kay Mooney Cox, "A Comparison of the Biblical and Native American Views of the Human Relationship with Nature" (Ph.D. diss., Graduate Theological Union, 1979).

15. See John Reumann, *Creation and New Creation* (Minneapolis: Augsburg, 1973).

16. Gösta Lindeskog, "The Theology of Creation in the Old and New Testaments," in *The Root of the Vine: Essays in Biblical Theology*, ed. Anton Fridrichsen (London: Dacre Press, 1953): 12.

17. Ibid., 12–13.

18. Santmire, *Brother Earth*, 90.

19. Santmire, *Travail of Nature*, 208.

20. Ibid., 202.

21. Ibid.

22. Paul M. Gregorios, "New Testament Foundations for Understanding the Creation," in *Tending the Garden: Essays on the Gospel and the Earth*, ed. Wesley Granberg-Michaelson (Grand Rapids: Eerdmans, 1987), 84.

23. Ibid., 85.

24. John G. Gibbs, *Creation and Redemption: A Study in Pauline Theology* (Leiden: Brill, 1971), 40. George Johnston ("οἰκουμένη and κόσμος in the New Testament," *New Testament Studies* 10 [1964]: 352–60) sheds light on the word study of Gk. *kosmos* as used in writings of the period and, specifically, Paul's use of the word. *Kosmos* has a multiplicity of meanings, including (a) *universe* (e.g., Matt. 13:35; Luke 11:50; John 17:24; Rom. 1:20; Eph. 1:4; Heb. 4:3; 1 Pet. 1:20; Rev. 13:8); (b) *earth, man's home,* or *mankind* itself (e.g., Mark 14:9; John 16:21; 1 Pet. 9); (c) *the cares, pleasures, and other interests of this time and space* (e.g., 1 Cor. 7:31, 33; 1 John 3:17); and (d) *the world as God's enemy, the dominion of the devil* (e.g., Gal. 4:3). Johnston fails to identify the particular meaning attached with Paul's use of *kosmos* in Romans 8, but others regard it as implying the universe in total.

25. Santmire, *Brother Earth*, 109.

26. Ibid.

27. Ibid.

28. Reumann, *Creation and New Creation*, 80.

29. Lindeskog, "Theology of Creation," 10–11.

30. Reumann, *Creation and New Creation*, 80–81.

31. Taylor, *New Creation.*

32. Ibid.

33. Santmire, *Brother Earth*, 109; see also Isaiah 11:6–8.

34. Maahs, "Theology."

35. Ibid.

36. Taylor, *New Creation.*

37. Santmire, *Brother Earth*, 125.

38. Hans Heinrich Schmid, "Creation, Righteousness, and Salvation: 'Creation Theology' as the Broad Horizon of Biblical Theology," in *Creation in the Old Testament*, ed. Bernhard W. Anderson (Philadelphia: Fortress, 1984), 112.

39. J. A. Ziesler, *The Meaning of Righteousness in Paul; A Linguistic and Theological Inquiry* (London: Cambridge University Press, 1972), 38.

40. Ibid., 1–2.

41. Ibid., 2.

42. Ibid., 3–4.

43. Ibid., 4.

44. 2 Peter 3:10–12.

45. Ezekiel 22:18–22.

46. Kenneth Barker, ed., *The NIV Study Bible: New International Version* (Grand Rapids: Zondervan, 1985), 1256.

47. Isaiah 1:21–22, 25, 26.

48. Malachi 3:2–3.

49. Matthew 13:40–43.

50. Revelation 21:7–9.

51. Genesis 6:5–13.

52. *Oxford Annotated Bible*, commentary on Psalm 104:35.

53. Paul Evdokimov, "Nature," *Scottish Journal of Theology* 18 (1965): 1–2.

General Index

Scripture Index

153